Wallace Welch

How to Become a

In Your Relationship

Let No One Move You from the Place God Put You

authorHOUSE™

1663 LIBERTY DRIVE, SUITE 200
BLOOMINGTON, INDIANA 47403
(800) 839-8640
WWW.AUTHORHOUSE.COM

First published by AuthorHouse 06/20/05

ISBN: 1-4208-3769-9 (sc)

Library of Congress Control Number: 2005904861

Printed in the United States of America
Bloomington, Indiana

This book is printed on acid-free paper.

For more information go to
www.HowtoBecomeAWinnerinyourrelationship.com

This book is dedicated to the members of World's Church of the Living God of Saint Lucie County, Florida

Acknowledgments

Thanks to Bishop W. C. Hunter

And the

World's Church of the Living God Ministries

Thanks to all, for the many years of dedication to the work of God.

Contents

Introduction

I would like to first thank God for allowing me to spend twenty-two years learning the wisdom of His word. Through His teaching, I have come to the conclusion that the relationship between man and woman is one of the most misunderstood institutions there is. The problems and circumstances that come along with a relationship have no respect of person, background, or religious belief. For instance, take a look at individuals who attend church and those who do not. Even though they both take different paths, many times, they end up with the same results. These results can produce negative effects which Christians seem to handle better with the help of God.

Ask yourself the following question: Could the almighty God have made a mistake in creating the woman for the man? He created both the man and the woman, and this relationship was first formed as a guide to those that followed. I ask once again, did God indeed make a mistake? I think not.

Today, there are many people attempting to instruct individuals about their relationships without God's wisdom. As a result, relationships seem to fail time and time again. I feel as though I have been inspired to reveal God's purpose set forth from the beginning. For His word is like good medicine, sometimes it's hard to take, but when mixed with someone you love, it goes down a lot better. Throughout this book, I'm going to mix the word of God with the wisdom given by God, and when you've reached the final page, you will have received the knowledge and understanding it takes to make you a *WINNER*.

This book is not only for christians
But for anyone willing to read with
an open mind

And follow God's instructions

Chapter 1
The Way, The Truth, And The Life

As a young man not knowing Christ, I remember lying in bed many nights dreaming about the perfect relationship. This desire must have been put within us by God, because why would I be thinking about a relationship when, as a young man, there were so many other things to think about. Not knowing why, I always looked up toward heaven not having any knowledge about church, the meaning of being saved, or that God even existed. Nevertheless, I continued to look toward heaven and dream one day that if I ever got married, I wanted God to bless me with the ideal relationship. I always knew in my heart it took a greater power to grant my desires. After seeing so many relationships end in disaster, I thought to myself, there has to be a better way. At that time, the only hope or chance any of us had would come from God because He must be the foundation upon which we must build our relationships.

I Corinthians 3:10 "According to the grace of God which is given unto me, as a wise masterbuilder, I have laid the foundation, and another buildeth thereon. But let every man take heed how he buildeth thereupon."

I Corinthians 3:11 "For other foundation can no man lay than that is laid, which is Jesus Christ."

Being the youngest in my family, I watched my older sisters and brothers go through ups and downs in their relationships. I said to myself, "I never want to be like that (leaning on my own understanding), I want to be different." I didn't want to get into a marriage where I have problem after problem, because I knew when problems exist, you can't function clearly. They will have an effect on your job performance, hobbies, sleep pattern, eating habits, and many other areas in your life. These changes happen not only to the person who's in a relationship but also the individual in search of someone, unless you choose to be alone.

The key is finding the right person. And, when you find that person, before you commit to anything, make sure you can truly love them. I'm talking about loving everything about that individual because one thing overlooked could bring about a bitter end.

You must understand that, at this point, I was only dreaming. But as the dream ended, I awoke to reality. I realized I was not married and only dating but yet it was still a relationship. The road I was on seemed to be heading down the same path everyone else was taking. Arguments and disagreements became a part of our weekly routine. It didn't matter what we did or how well we got along, it was as if the spirit of confusion was all around. To this very day, couples that really love each other can let the smallest matter get out of control. Some feel as though they have no communication with their husband or wife unless it's something to complain about. For many relationships, this has become a way of life.

One day, a friend told me that *JESUS CHRIST* could make a difference. She was sure about what God could do. Therefore, one Sunday morning, she invited me out to church. Now, as I look back, this was by far the best thing anyone had done for me.

It's amazing how good life can be when you are thinking correctly. I started attending church three times a week. Within that period, I accepted *JESUS* as my Lord and Savior. I got married shortly after, and I was sure church was going to be the *magic remedy* that made everything right.

My involvement in the work of the ministry and the work of God helped me stay focused during the beginning stages of my marriage. I was hearing the word of God, and at the same time, having ups and downs in my relationship like everyone else. So church, in the beginning, did not seem like the correct way to go at marriage either, but I hung in there. I kept looking to God and to the heavens from which cometh my help. Truly, my help came from the Lord who made the heavens and the earth. As I obeyed the word, and the closer I got to God, the better my relationship got. The more I trusted in God and the more I got involved in His work, the better my relationship became. The more I obeyed what I was instructed to do in the ministry, the better my relationship became. A pattern was definitely taking shape.

Romans 10:17 "So then faith cometh by hearing, and hearing by the word of God."

The more I grew in my relationship with God, the less I focused on the negative things going on within my personal relationship itself. I began to change first as a man. I started to feel like I had control of my life and the marriage. My thinking was different. For once, I felt I was in the position God wanted me to be. I learned that having the right person brings about the right spirit and the right spirit brings love, joy, peace, longsuffering, gentleness, goodness, faith, meekness, and temperance; for all of these there is no law. Before you can love someone in a relationship, you must first love yourself. Change the things about you that you don't like before you try to get someone else to accept the way you are. Sometimes the things we don't like about ourselves are not easy to change. With some areas in our life, we will need God's help to correct problems.

II Corinthian 5:17 "Therefore if any man be in Christ, he is a new creature: old things passed away; behold, all things are become new."

I stand today after twenty-nine years of marriage and still find it to be a challenge, but with God's help, we make it each and every day. I will be the first to admit that no one on this planet is perfect according to the Bible. For this reason, we all need help from the Lord because with Him, all things are possible.

I've spent the last twenty-two years counseling, giving advice, and teaching married couples within the church. I've also instructed couples that were not in church because I know the word of God will have an effect on whoever receives it. With the wisdom and knowledge of God, it can work for anyone: the saved man, the lost man, and the unbelievers if you're strong enough to accept it.

The word of God is powerful. It has the ability to change a man and have a positive influence on his life. Therefore, I did not turn anyone away when they had a relationship dilemma. I believe there's not a problem you're facing that can't be solved through the word of God. Your life, your situation, and your relationship will become better, that is, if you're willing to listen and obey. It's been proven time and time again that any man who listens and takes heed to the instructions God has given will surely be blessed.

Proverbs 8:33 "Hear instruction, and be wise, and refuse it not."

Proverbs 8:34 "Blessed is the man that heareth me, watching daily at my gates, waiting at the posts of my doors."

Proverbs 8:35 "For whoso findeth me findeth life, and shall obtain favour of the Lord."

The choice is ultimately up to you whether to listen and obey. It's definitely a tall order. Just take a hard look around at our society today. You find everything going on. People are building new homes, buying new cars, obtaining new jobs, and starting new businesses. The world is ever changing but the main thing God set in place before all of this was the relationship between man and woman which is the thing that seems to fail the most. Through God's wisdom, we have a hope that if we are willing to accept it and believe it, we can change it.

Family life is the most important thing there is and should be before anything you possess. Yet still, we are not willing to give our all to make it work. From the beginning of time to the present, look at what has happened to relationships throughout the years. They've strayed away from the relationship between man and woman first established by God in the beginning to very few good marriages, unions between man and man, and unions between woman and woman.

Everyone is trying to find something to help them reach the ultimate goal that God put before us. If you really think about it for a moment, it's quite difficult to understand why it's so hard for some to see that God didn't intend for a man to be with another man or a woman to be with another woman. The marriage breakup between man and woman ending in one divorce after another sends a bad message that God made a mistake. Why is it so hard to see? Well, because whether man and man, woman and woman, or man and woman, we are all searching for that which God has put within us: that ultimate goal of being happy with someone we love and who loves us in return.

We are going to keep searching for that connection God established from the beginning until we fill the void. This is why you find people trying to obtain happiness through relationships with dogs, cats, birds, and all kinds of creatures to replace the connection God placed between man and woman. Throughout life, we will continue to search and find different detours on the road to ultimate happiness.

I am here to tell you that true happiness comes from the relationship between man and woman as God created it. You may say, "I've tried the man, I've tried the woman, and it's just not working; it's just not for me; it's always something." This is because you have not given God's advice, counseling, wisdom, or knowledge a true chance. You can say, "I've gone to church, I've done this, I've done that." I still say, "You have not given God a chance."

Within the pages of this book, you will find out how God intended it to be from the beginning. I know if you receive the message in this book, the knowledge of God will make you a *winner* in your relationship. For once in your life, take heed to what is being said and give God a chance. I'm a firm believer that there is no other way but the way God has laid out so clearly and simply. He will never change. I decided to go the way in which God has guided me, and I encourage you to do the same.

The wonderful truth is that God loves you and He cares for you. Probably by now, the reason you picked up this book is because you want to be a *winner* in your relationship. Therefore, I encourage you to read this book and stay with it until the final page. I'm sure with the knowledge and wisdom He has given me to share, you can become a *winner*. God wants you to prosper and be happy above all things.

II Peter 3:9 "The Lord is not slack concerning his promise, as some men count slackness; but is long-suffering to us-ward, not willing that any should perish, but all should come to repentance."

Sometimes, we get the understanding from many that He only cares about the believers, but you must realize that even before we were converted, God had compassion on us also. I'm saying today the word of God can be of great benefit to you. The instructions of God are here to help you enjoy life to the fullest, which He intended for man to do from the beginning.

II Peter 2:20 "For if after they have escaped the pollutions of the world through the knowledge of the Lord and savior Jesus Christ, they are again entangled therein, and overcome, the latter end is worse with them than the beginning."

That means, regardless if you are lost or saved, in church or out, through God's knowledge you can enjoy a wonderful life and escape many of the trials, hardships and circumstances in the world. Knowledge alone will not get you into heaven, but it will allow you to enjoy a little heaven here on earth.

God created man and knows all about him. This being true, He knew exactly what it took for you to make it when He wrote these instructions.

Psalms 48:14 "For this God is our God for ever and ever: he will be our guide even unto death."

God had us in mind when He created all the beauty you behold. Now, I think it's time you start thinking about yourself. I believe we all have equal opportunity as believers and non-believers. The only difference between the two is that we as believers have Christ within us to lead and guide us into all truth. Sometimes, believers are going to make a better decision but you will have the same opportunity if you are willing to follow God's plan He so carefully laid out for us.

The key to becoming a *winner* is not whether you are saved or lost; it's how well you follow God's instructions described in the passages below.

Matthew 7:24 "Therefore whosoever heareth these sayings of mine, and doeth them, I will liken him unto a wise man, which built his house upon a rock."

Matthew 7:25 "And the rain descended, and the floods came, and the winds blew, and beat upon that house; and it fell not: for it was founded upon a rock."

Matthew 7:26 "And every one that heareth these sayings of mine, and doeth them not, shall be likened unto a foolish man, which built his house upon the sand:"

Matthew 7:27 "And the rain descended, and the floods came, and winds blew and beat upon that house; and it fell: and great was the fall of it."

God is merciful, as you can see. It doesn't matter whether you attend church or not, according to the scripture. What matters is that you hear what God has to say and obey it. A saved person can attend church and not follow instructions making their life appear in the *natural* world as that of an unbeliever of *Christ*.

James 1:22 "But be ye doers of the word and not hearers only, deceiving your own selves."

James 1:23 "For if any be a hearer of the word, and not a doer, he is like unto a man beholding his natural face in a glass:"

James 1:24 "For he beholdeth

Himself, and goeth his way, and straightway forgetteth what manner of man he was."

James 1:25 "But whoso looketh into the perfect law of liberty, and continueth therein, he being not a forgetful hearer, but a doer of the work, this man shall be blessed in his deed."

That's how you get results. God's word will show us the way by giving us the truth to get the most out of life here on earth. There's going to be many who disagree with what I'm saying, but I just want to let you know that we are living in troublesome times. We need to draw nigh to God and follow His instructions a little more closely.

As the book of Matthew states, one house fell and the other stood only because one followed God's instructions and the other refused. Hearing instructions alone will not change a person's life. Many know what God has said but will not follow what they know. They must not only hear but also do what they have been instructed. The man whose house collapsed was at fault not because he failed to labor but because he did not lay the proper foundation. The shifting sand represents human opinion and doctrines of men rather than the instructions of God. Many have worked hard for everything they've built over the years; how one can take the chance of it collapsing by leaning on his or her own understanding is beyond me.

When we become a believer of Christ, sometimes we feel we're so much better than others, but God did not make us, like the sun, big and so out of touch with people that it puts a distance between the saved and the lost. He intended for the believers to be a light in view so others can see that He makes the difference. By them seeing our light, they may decide to give God a chance.

Matthew 5:14 "Ye are the light of the world. A city that is set on a hill cannot be hid."

Matthew 5:15 "Neither do men light a candle, and put it under a bushel, but on a candlestick; and it giveth light unto all that are in the house."

Matthew 5:16 "Let your light so shine before men, that they may see your good works and glorify your Father which is in heaven."

There should not be such a difference in how we look at the God who created heaven and earth. Whether you acknowledge it or not, we all benefit from God's goodness everyday. He has no respect of person. Regardless of what path you've taken in life, to be alive is something to give thanks for. To God be the glory. To wake up each day and be given all of the good every other person on the face of this earth receives, you must first begin to believe that He has to love us all. It does not rain for me and not you because I am in Christ, neither does the sun shine for me and not for you because I am in Christ.

Matthew 5:45 "That ye be the children of your Father which is in heaven: for he maketh his sun to rise on the evil and on the good, and senteth rain on the just and the unjust."

The rise in divorces and problems before marriage are leaving many to think it's impossible to have a wonderful relationship. Many who are not divorced feel as though they have failed because they are married but are unhappy. I know you're asking yourself, "Is there really a solid plan to a winning relationship in the stages of dating or in the institution of marriage?" The answer is *Yes*! But, to accomplish what you set out to do is like a million-mile journey where you *must* start the first mile in the right direction. What's the first mile? The first mile is consulting our God for instruction. Marriage is a long journey due to the fact that it's a long learning process because we, as humans, will be forever changing. God can keep our minds renewed day by day which will allow us to adjust to the changes.

Proverbs 4:13 "Take fast hold of instruction; let her not go: keep her; for she is thy life."

Proverbs 12:1 "Whoso loveth instruction loveth knowledge: but he that hateth reproof is brutish."

Proverbs 9:9 "Give instruction to a wise man, and he will be yet wiser: teach a just man, and he will increase in learning."

Proverbs 9:10 "The fear of the Lord is the beginning of wisdom: and the knowledge of the Holy is understanding."

A beautiful relationship can be established by living as the Bible states. I believe this information is simple, the way God intended it to be. Many are teaching above people, they will agree with what's being said but don't *really* understand the concept. Nevertheless, they are left to embark upon life's journey leaning on their own understanding. Seek God's counsel, and not only will you be heading in the right direction, but you will make good time while doing so.

Proverbs 3:5 "Trust in the Lord with all thine heart; and lean not unto thine own understanding."

The spoken words of God have made the blind to see, the lame to walk, the deaf to hear; surely, they have the power to make you a *winner* in your relationship. You can become a *winner* and the person you are with can become a *winner* also, which will lead to a happy home. Everyone in the relationship must do their part. I know the question you want to ask is, "Is it possible to be a *winner* without the other?" Yes! God's advice will change you as an individual first.

I am but a man, but I think I also have the spirit of God. Follow me through this book as I am led by the spirit within me.

Chapter 2
God Created Man

A llow me to start by saying that I salute all men with great respect. At this very moment, I am extremely excited to share with you what the almighty God had planned for us. Believe me when I speak about the man, it brings me great joy because I am a true man after God's own heart. As this chapter unfolds, you will see that God created man to be a unique being with a purpose. Having created him in His own image and after His likeness, there was none like him. Everything God created was good. He believed in us from the beginning and gave us complete control over all He created.

Genesis 1:26 "And God said, Let us make man in our image, after our likeness: and let them have dominion over the fish of the sea, and over the fowl of the air, and over the cattle, and over all the earth, and over every creeping thing that creepeth upon the earth."

Genesis 1:27 "So God created man in his own image, in the image of God created he him; male and female created he them."

Remember this is the beginning when He created male and female. Therefore, God knew His intentions for them. They were smart together and had power over all of God's material creations.

To some it will appear that God made the male and female equal, but at this point, He had not defined their purpose.

Genesis 2:5 *"And every plant of the field before it was in the earth, and every herb of the field before it grew: for the Lord God had not caused it to rain upon the earth, and there was not a man to till the ground."*

According to the latter part of the above verse, God was in need of someone to work and maintain that which He created. God had the answer right away and this began the creation of man. God put a great deal of thought into creating man for He knew his purpose.

Genesis 2:7 "And the Lord God formed man of the dust of the ground, and breathed into his nostrils the breath of life; and man became a living soul."

God is Lord and the Creator of Man. This represents the potter at work, setting the design and pattern for the perfection of man. First, God created man a body from the materials of the earth. Next, He gave man a heart and breathed "*the breath of life*" into his nostrils making him a "*living soul.*" Man, now having physical being, could possess the earth, make it serve him, and rule the other creatures within it.

Psalm 8:5 "For thou hast made him a little lower than the angels, and hast crowned him with glory and honor."

Psalm 8:6 "Thou madest him to have dominion over the works of thy hands; thou hast put all things under his feet:"

Psalm 8:7 "All sheep and oxen, yea, and the beasts of the field;"

Psalm 8:8 "The fowl of the air and the fish of the sea, and whatsoever passeth through the paths of the seas."

Only in obedience can man be what he truly is. God's word in which he lives offers him the knowledge that lifts him above the rest of creation.

Man has a loving God who is committed to supplying his every need. The love that God has for mankind exceeds our natural understanding. The key for man is to live by God's word which will unlock the door to the many treasures within this life. God's word is not meant to bring about added burden on the souls and hearts of men but more so to point man in the way of happiness.

When man refuses to follow God's word and man refuses to enter the relationship created to fulfill his purpose, it gives way to him seeking to find justification for his existence within himself. If God is not leading and guiding a man, it is much easier for him to get off track. He was not created to murder without a cause or rape for no reason at all, these things and other sad actions happen when man is trying to find his place without God.

Today, instead of man seeking to enter a true relationship with God, he seeks to find the meaning of his destiny through relationships with things in the world. As a result, bondage and frustration characterize his life, making way for evil to enter into his heart and mind.

Adam, being obedient to God in the beginning, He created a special place where he would live. God called it the *"Garden of Eden"*. "Eden" means *delight*. This was Adam's first home. The garden was beautiful to behold, having everything man needed to survive. He gave man, within his makeup, the ability to appreciate things that are pleasant to look upon just as God appreciates beauty.

Genesis 2:15 "And the Lord God took the man, and put him into the garden of Eden to dress it and to keep it."

God required man to be responsible for what was given to him. The garden needed upkeep; this was man's first job. He had to work in the garden and live off his work. Man was not designed for someone to take care of him but for the purpose of taking care of his surroundings.

In the midst of the garden was the tree of the knowledge of good and evil. God placed this object of testing where man would live, but man failed the test by disobeying God's instruction not to eat of the fruit of this one tree.

Genesis 2:16 *"And the Lord God commanded the man, saying, Of every tree of the garden thou mayest freely eat:"*

Genesis 2:17 *"But of the tree of the knowledge of good and evil, thou shalt not eat of it: for in the day that thou eatest thereof thou shalt surely die."*

God had created man and met his every need. The only thing in the garden man was instructed ***not*** to do was eat of the tree of the knowledge of good and evil. There was no reason to disobey and eat the forbidden fruit.

II Corinthians 12:9 "And he said unto me, My grace is sufficient for thee: for my strength is made perfect in weakness."

Adam had the mind of Christ in thinking everything created was good. I believe he had no knowledge of evil. God gave Adam clear instructions as to what would happen if he ate of the forbidden tree. The instructions God gave in the Bible will stand after this earth has passed away. Therefore, it will benefit us to follow God's advice.

Man was created alone without the woman, which indicates man is a special creation of God unlike any of His earlier creations. All other creatures were created in pairs having a male and a female to reproduce "after its kind." This was extremely important. God knew in the beginning that man was able to deal with whatever responsibility he was given. The same applies today. Every man has the ability to handle the task put before him.

Deuteronomy 11:13 "And it shall come to pass, if ye shall hearken diligently unto my commandments which I command you this day, to love the Lord your God, and to serve him with all your heart and with all your soul,"

Deuteronomy 11:14 "That I will give you the rain of your land in due season, the first and the latter rain, that thou mayest gather in thy corn, and thy wine, and thine oil."

Deuteronomy 11:15 "And I will send grass in thy fields for thy cattle, that thou mayest eat and be full."

Deuteronomy 11:16 "Take heed to yourselves, that your heart be not deceived, and ye turn aside, and serve other gods, and worship them;"

Deuteronomy 11:17 "And then the Lord's wrath be kindled against you, and he shut up the heaven, that there be no rain, and that the land yield not her fruit; and lest ye perish quickly from off the good land which the Lord giveth you."

When Adam followed God's instruction, everything he had need of, God supplied it. God feels the same way about man today, and He is ready to meet our every need.

As a man, God has put you at the mountaintop and no one has the ability to bring you down but yourself. You should not let anything or anyone move you from the place God put you in. If you are at the bottom of the mountain, for whatever reason, look up, get up, think up, and return to the top. When you get to the top, stay up. We are all different in one way or another, but as men, we are all great when viewed from heaven.

All of the things God wanted for man are present in the world. If you are not careful, you may not see good when it comes your way. We are more than conquerors through Him who loves us. Success or failure starts in your mind.

I know the spirit of God has led me throughout the years. I do not claim to be perfect, and I will be the first to admit that no one else is perfect either.

I John 1:8 "If we say that we have no sin, we deceive ourselves, and the truth is not in us."

I John 1:9 "If we confess our sins, he is faithful and just to forgive us our sins, and to cleanse us from all unrighteousness."

I John 1:10 "If we say that we have not sinned, we make him a liar, and his word is not in us."

This is one of my life experiences. As a young man, I knew very little about how to preserve a marriage. My wife had a full-time job before we got married. I had always known her to be a hard worker. Now that we were married, I quickly started planning everything without God's help. My first thought was we could have more if both of us worked. "This is going to be great," I said to myself. Visions of a new car or two, a better place to live, acquiring new things, and having more money in my pockets entered into my mind. I began to wonder if I was the only one thinking like this or if my wife was thinking the same way. It's amazing to me how money can creep in and first control your thoughts and then every aspect of your relationship.

Matthew 6:24 "No man can serve two masters: for either he will hate the one, and love the other; or else he will hold to the one, and despise the other. Ye cannot serve god and mammon."

After we got married, all I could think about was having more. Right from the start, money became the focal point of our marriage. When a man thinks he owns something, it starts to own him. Therefore, it then begins to control him rather than him controlling it.

Instead of saying, "What can I do for my marriage?" I was wondering, "What can the marriage do for me?" Many things in life have the ability to get switched around when man disregards God's instructions.

Just about everything we purchase comes with instructions within the package, and when we follow them, we get the best results. Even though the pieces look different and go in different places, they fit well together. Knowing this, why would we attempt to establish a relationship with someone else without consulting God first? Everyone has a mind of their own and with the capability to agree or disagree; without God's instruction, the battle is on!

Proverbs 3:7 "Be not wise in thine own eyes: fear the Lord, and depart from evil."

Proverbs 3:8 "It shall be health to thy navel, and marrow to thy bones."

So as my story continues, we began our first day as husband and wife. Everything was okay; we both started the day by going to work. When I came home, she was in the bed, there was no dinner on the table, the house was not clean, and everything else was out of order. Not a problem, I was thinking, it is only the first day. The second day held much of the same, and at this point, I was wondering what was going on. The third day, she did not get out of bed for work. From that day forth, and now twenty-nine years later, she has not worked another day. I did not realize it at the time but believe it or not, I look back now and feel that was the way God wanted it to happen in our marriage. There were many things that happened over the years that I could not understand, but today, I realize everything that happened was in the will of God. This book runs parallel with my life.

Some people think when the man works and the woman stays at home, that's the *old-fashioned* way of life or the outdated way. I must admit you are right on the first part, *old fashioned,* because it was planned from the beginning. On the second part, you're wrong because there's nothing that God established that will become outdated. If it is *old fashioned or outdated,* I will take it any day because it works.

I think the Lord guided me over the years to demonstrate how the plan works. When a man is the head of the house, God's plan can take its course. It will not work successfully any other way.

God appointed me head over all things for the benefit of the family. He has blessed me to be wise and skillful to infuse my family with my life and character.

In my house, I take care of all the responsibilities. As God gave Adam dominion over everything He created, I have rule over my house. **Watch out!** Be careful what you think, I'm only trying to follow God's plan.

As a man, life is wonderful because I know who I am. There is no need to walk around saying, "I'm the man" or "I'm the head of the house." I am not a man because my wife says I am or because I pay the bills. I am who I am by the grace of God. I have taken the position that the Lord has given me. Therefore, the things which are done in my relationship, I do them unto the Lord.

When God makes you the head of the household, what is there to boast about? You can invite me into your home for dinner and put me in any seat. It does not matter because I know wherever I sit that becomes the head of the table only because I know my place in God's marvelous plan.

If things go wrong within your relationship, you tend to look down on yourself or blame the wife when you don't have knowledge and understanding from the Bible. As head of the home, a man must lead by example. He should be the first to say, "I'm sorry" or "I didn't handle the situation well." You must remember being over a household is like running a company. A man must first be able to manage his own life. A man who manages his own life poorly is not capable of giving proper leadership to a household. You are the boss. When things are out of order, it's up to you to correct the problem. If the problem goes unresolved, you may lose an employee. No, you do not have to own a business to know what I am talking about. You are the CEO of your family and all assets you've acquired over time. As a man, do not be afraid of taking risks because there is no such thing as zero risks when in a leadership position. God created us for that purpose, and we must see it through at any cost.

God knew what He was doing by putting man in charge because the more he takes on, the stronger he becomes. Like a weightlifter when he adds five pounds to the bar, he works with that for a while and when he becomes stronger, he adds more weight. Do you see where I am going with this? We are no exception. God designed us so that our minds function the same way.

My life is a prime example. From a spiritual prospective, I started in the ministry first as one of the brethren. Next, I became a deacon, then a minister, and I am now a pastor. The same pattern is shown in nature: First, I was an employee, then I became a manager, and I am now a business owner hoping to one day start a high-tech manufacturing training school. When a man takes on more responsibility, he will be willing to face greater challenges.

You can refuse to fulfill your purpose, but you will end up hurting yourself. Whatever you allow, God will allow, because He's given us freewill to do as we please. That freewill has gotten us into trouble, like Adam in his situation. But, no matter how far we go in the wrong direction, the Lord will always be there waiting if we have a change of heart.

By Adam's sin, death entered into the world. Because of him, all men sin and die. Through the disobedience of one man, we were all made sinners. Adam's one trespass branded us with the judgment of condemnation passed upon us and death to reign over us. God has given us a way out which can help us overcome anything through His wisdom and knowledge.

There is none before Adam, for he is the first man. There is none between Adam and Christ because Christ is the second Adam. There is none after Christ, for He is the last Adam. Adam was therefore the one to come which is Christ. With Christ, we can take our place once again, having the opportunity to live in paradise through Him.

Romans 5:17 "For if by one man's offense death reigned by one; much more they which receive abundance of grace and of the gift of righteousness shall reign in life by one, Jesus Christ."

Romans 5:18 "Therefore as by the offense of one judgment came upon all men to condemnation; even so by the righteousness of one the free gift came upon all men unto justification of life."

Romans 5:19 "For as by one man's disobedience many were made sinners, so by the obedience of one shall many be made righteous."

Romans 5:20 "Moreover the law entered, that the offense might abound. But where sin abounded, grace did much more abound:"

Romans 5:21 "That as sin hath reigned unto death, even so might grace reign through righteousness unto eternal life by Jesus Christ our Lord."

Yet, in spite of the fall of man, the promise of Christ must still be regarded as in the image of God. Not because of what he is in himself but because of what Christ is for him and because of what he is in Christ. In Christ is seen the true meaning of the covenant which God sought to make with man.

James 3:9 "Therewith bless we God, even the Father; and therewith curse we men, which are made after the similitude of God."

For the unfaithfulness of man does not nullify the faithfulness of God toward him. Therefore, in the sight of God, man, seen both in the saved or lost aspects of life, is more valuable than the whole realm of nature. The finding of the lost man is worth the most painful search and complete sacrifice on His part. The almighty God will love nothing more than for all men to stand strong and begin a lasting relationship with Him. God doesn't want even one man wondering about as though he has no hope.

Every man is a special creation of God in spite of how society has labeled many of them. What every man has become is no fault of God because He made all men the same. We all are products of our environment. We will continue on a reckless course unless we turn to God for guidance. If you are blind to God's plan as a man, how can you lead someone else? Your blindness as a leader will cause all those who follow you to suffer.

Matthew 9:36 "But when he saw the multitudes, he was moved with compassion on them, because they fainted, and were scattered aboard, as sheep having no shepherd."

Matthew 9:37 "Then saith he unto his disciples, The harvest truly is plenteous but the labourers are few;"

Jesus Christ is the true image of God and thus the image of a *true* man. He is both a unique individual and the inclusive representative of the whole race. His achievements and victory mean freedom and life for all mankind. He fulfills the covenant in which God bestows on man his true destiny. In Christ, by faith, man finds himself changing back into the likeness of God. This gives us full conformity to His image.

II Corinthians 3:18 "But we all, with open face beholding as in a glass the glory of the Lord, are changed into the same image from glory to glory, even as by the Spirit of the Lord."

Thanks be to God we have a true man to follow, one that followed the guide which God laid out for him from the beginning without failure. We must have the mind of Christ. He is the firstborn of many brethren. With God's word, it can be done.

He was sent here for that purpose to show that the road to becoming a *winner* may not be easy but it is achievable. You may lose a few battles along the way, but circumstances don't make you a loser.

These are the words of Jesus: **"WITH MEN, THIS IS IMPOSSIBLE; BUT WITH GOD, ALL THINGS ARE POSSIBLE."**

Chapter 3
God Created Woman

To the woman: I stand and take my hat off, for I honor you each day. Let no one tell you that you are not special. Always walk with your head up because God loves you. You were also created in the image of God, regardless of what culture or background you are from; no one had anything to do with how you are, for it was God who shaped and molded you. He put man in a deep sleep whereas he could not interfere while He created you. God fashioned the woman in beauty, gentleness, kindness, and all the other wonderful things that He is, as you were created after His likeness. Don't be what someone else wants you to be. God had a purpose for you, and it is very important that you know and understand that purpose.

Genesis 5:2 *"Male and female created he them; and blessed them, and called their name Adam, in the day when they were created."*

When God blessed them, He did not only bestow His blessing upon them but also assigned them separate functions as man and woman.

God knew His objective when He created the male and the female. He saw that in the right order, they are capable of not only working together but also staying together. What was seen by God is hard to comprehend as it is reflected very little in today's society. Many today change husbands and wives like they change automobiles. Sometimes individuals don't make the first payment and some marriages don't make it a month. You must remember there is someone who is totally well-matched for you, so don't settle for the first person who comes along.

When God created the various animals that would walk and live on the earth, there was a male and a female of each kind. Unlike these other creatures, Adam was incomplete as he did not have a companion. God was aware of Adam's loneliness. Man was put in a paradise and given dominion over all of God's creation. With everything the Lord gave him, man was yet lacking. Without the woman, he will always lack in certain areas of his life. No other creature or substance can fill the void in his life better than a woman.

Genesis 2:20 "And Adam gave names to all cattle, and to the fowl of the air, and to every beast of the field; but for Adam there was not found a help meet for him."

God then gives the purpose of the woman in stating Adam's need for a "*help meet.*"

In creating a help meet for the man, God performed the first surgical operation. He put Adam to sleep, removed one of his ribs, and closed the wound with the surrounding flesh. The woman was made from a rib which God took from the man. It was taken from his side, not from his head to rule over him and not from his feet to show inferiority. The woman's position was established by God taking the rib from the man's side. And at his side is where she belongs. I don't want my wife riding in the backseat of the car when I'm driving or sleeping on the floor when I'm in the bed, because she belongs wherever I am.

Ecclesiastes 1:9 "The thing that hath been, it is that which shall be; and that which is done is that which shall be done: and there is no new thing under the sun."

Genesis 2:22 "And the rib, which the Lord God had taken from man, made he a woman, and brought her unto the man."

We must understand that woman was created as man's helper in life. She is to assist man in fulfilling his purpose. The woman being a helper to the man should not be considered as a position of inferiority. God intended for man and woman to work together with a common purpose in life. When someone is a helper, it doesn't mean they are weak or of less importance, for God is our help in the time of need.

Psalm 115:9 "O Israel, trust thou in the Lord: he is their help and their shield."

According to the Bible, the woman is not inferior to the man. She has a purpose and position in the relationship with the man. When a woman is a helper and a supporter, she is fulfilling the will of God which allows Him to help the man through her. Therefore, she is God's helper in meeting man's needs. She is indeed a special creation and should always be viewed as a creation of beauty. Praise God, for you are wonderfully made.

I have always believed that all women are special in their own way. When my daughters were young girls, I never allowed them to have skates, a bicycle, or anything that could possibly put a scar on them from falling by accident. I know many times they would sneak and skate with their friends or ride someone else's bicycle on an occasion. When they got caught in the act, I had no problem explaining why I made that decision. It is not a pretty thing to watch a beautiful woman with damaged teeth or a bad scar from a fall that took place during her childhood. With my son, he was born to be tough. Therefore, he was allowed to skate and ride his bicycle. A scrape or a scar on him did not affect me as much as it did with my daughters. There was something special about my girls, and I wanted to protect them as much as I could while they were small. I knew one day they would grow up and be young ladies who could be proud of the beauty that God gave them.

One day, I went out of town on a business trip. While I was away, my wife and kids planned a surprise party congratulating me on the success of my business venture. I arrived home that evening. Everyone in the house was excited and began congratulating me concerning the trip. At that moment, I was overwhelmed. As I was looking around at the decorations, I noticed one of the girls was missing. I asked my wife where she was; everyone in the house got quiet. Then I saw her come from around the corner. The thing that I feared the most had happened; she fell while riding her brother's bike. The right side of her face, her right arm, and right leg were badly marred. Needless to say, the party ended very quickly as silence filled the room.

To this very day, my then babies and now young ladies are very thankful that I protected them the way I did. I think that a woman's beauty is very special to God. He blessed the woman with that distinctive quality. The Bible states that Solomon had seven hundred wives, princesses, and three hundred concubines. He had many women only because they were all astonishing to him. But what Solomon did not comprehend was that God made all women special and different. If Solomon could have married every woman on the planet, he would have found something special about each one of them.

God gave Solomon a wise and an understanding heart, so that there were none like him before him, neither after him shall any arise like unto him.

Read and try to see through the eyes of a wise man that had great understanding.

And Solomon wrote:

Songs of Solomon 7:1 "How beautiful are thy feet with shoes, O prince's daughter! The joints of thy thighs are like jewels, the work of the hands of a cunning workman."

Songs of Solomon 7:2 "Thy naval is like a round goblet, which wanteth no liquor: thy belly is like a heap of wheat set about with lilies."

Songs of Solomon 7:3 "Thy two breasts are like two young roes that are twins."

Songs of Solomon 7:4 "Thy neck is a tower of ivory; thine eyes like the fishpools in Heshbon, by the gate of Bathrabbim: thy nose is as the tower of Lebanon which looketh toward Damascus."

Songs of Solomon 7:5 "Thine head upon thee is like Carmel, and the hair of thine head like purple; the King is held in the galleries."

Songs of Solomon 7:6 "How fair and how pleasant art thou, O love, for delights!"

Songs of Solomon 7:7 "This thy stature is like to a palm tree, and thy breasts to clusters of grapes."

Songs of Solomon 7:8 "I said, I will go up to the palm tree, I will take hold of the boughs thereof: now also thy breasts shall be as clusters of the vine, and the smell of thy nose like apples;"

Songs of Solomon 7:9 "And the roof of thy mouth like the best wine for my beloved, that goeth down sweetly, causing the lips of those that are asleep to speak."

To the woman, I say, man does not function well without you. God created you because man needed not only a companion but also a helper. A woman who is a helper to her husband will be with him longer than a woman that only wants him as a companion. A man will strive for the top, and he will become greater if the woman he is with believes in him. But many women will say, what about my needs? God has already taken care of that by a design within the plan. The man that you're with will give you more than enough in return. Remain in your place, and don't let the modern times change who you are meant to be in God's plan.

Having the spirit of faith, I believe the woman should not take on the more physical or aggressive responsibilities. God designed the man to handle such responsibilities including but not limited to protecting and taking care of the woman. For a woman's strength lies within caring and tenderness, the *softer side of life*.

Men, in this day and time, will think better, look better, feel better, and live longer if they have someone suitable to help meet their needs. Adam lived to be nine hundred and thirty years old. Could it be that in the beginning Eve had no greater task than to help Adam and take care of him? Now, having said that, how long will **your** man live?

As a woman, you must remember a *good man* cannot do without you. God created you to be suitable for the man. Therefore, don't cut yourself short in seeking alternative forms to fill the gap.

Your focus should be toward the needs of the man, and you should not allow anything or anyone to prohibit you from being a good helper to the man you chose. Looking out for him is more important than looking good for him. Some may disagree with that point, but you judge for yourself which will last the longest. I hereby dedicate the following poem to you with encouragement to be all God created you to be.

~~~~In Honor Of The Woman~~~~

Be all you can be for your beauty is for all to see.

I believe you will make all things right if you surrender to the will of God with delight.

He is wonderful in all His ways and He teaches you to watch and pray.

You must live one day at a time and give with love in mind.

You must accept your role in life without grumbling and strife.

God gave you a job to help your mate for this is your eternal state.

The Lord brings joy and peace because your trials will never cease.

You will be ever learning as knowledge will increase.

Don't let anyone stop you from giving and loving more because you are stronger than anyone gives you credit for.

God gave woman a place where she may flourish and bring forth His goodness as she protects and nourishes.

So believe in the source that created you, it is He that gives instructions that will guide you through.

The creator has wonderfully designed you with man in mind and His wisdom and knowledge will stand until the end of time.

So take the challenge with an open mind and allow God to give you joy divine.

Fulfill the purpose which God created you for and He shall give you the desires of your heart forevermore.

Begin your journey by taking heed and with God's knowledge you can succeed.

THE MORE KNOWLEDGE REVEALED TO ME AND THE MORE I UNDERSTAND, THE MORE I WISH WE COULD ALL START OVER AGAIN.

Chapter 4
God Created The First Marriage

We must go back to the beginning to see what was established as the perfect marriage which was designed to last forever. God's creation of Adam and Eve indicates the unique relationship of a husband and wife. As God looked down the corridors of life, He saw the church, and at the time, there was nothing greater than the marriage between man and woman. In the mind of God, the institution of marriage was a divine illustration of His love for the church. God's plan for marriage is so perfect that it serves as a portrait of the relationship between Him and His people, and the beauty of it symbolizes all the wonderful things He expects for the church.

Ephesians 5:22 "Wives, submit yourselves unto your own husband, as unto the Lord."

Ephesians 5:23 "For the husband is the head of the wife, even as Christ is the head of the church: and he is the savior of the body."

Ephesians 5:24 "Therefore as the church is subject unto Christ, so let the wives be to their own husbands in every thing."

Ephesians 5:25 "Husbands, love your wives, even as Christ also loved the church, and gave himself for it."

A marriage is very special. Can you imagine how beautiful it would be for a man to love his wife without thought of receiving any love in return? How many of us sit in church every week not obeying what Christ commands us to do but still expect Him to love and forgive us time and time again? Just as Christ gave Himself for the church, there should be no sacrifice a husband is not willing to make for his wife.

When the almighty God looks down from heaven to see the institution which He compared to the church, it must be somewhat disappointing. Marriage is the foundation of our society. The church represents marriage and marriage reflects the church. When you see the breakdown of marriage, you will also see the destruction of the church. God loves the church and laid down His life for it. If a man chooses to be a husband, he should be willing to lay down whatever he thinks is important for the well being of his family.

St. John 15:13 "Greater love hath no man than this, that a man lay down his life for his friends."

God made it clear that we as men must love our wives because it represents His love for the church. When viewed as God planned it, the church and the marriage should stand until the end of time. You must understand that there are many churches that claim they are serving God but are totally out of the realm as believers. By being out of the realm of God, outside factors may come into play and begin to affect the atmosphere of a ministry. But a ministry built upon the foundation of Christ can only be destroyed from the inside. This principle also applies to the marriage. If there is going to be a separation, it will come on behalf of the husband or the wife and not an outside influence. When we are committed to Christ, it is our decision to walk away. We find so many married couples today who blame the breakup of the marriage on someone else when, in reality, only we can make the decision to walk away.

The first wedding on the earth took place in the *Garden of Eden.* Our loving Father presents to the man the bride which He created. You must understand this is the only bride He gives to man. God created her to meet all of Adam's needs. He knew exactly what Adam wanted, and as a result, He created the perfect mate. Today, we have a much greater challenge to face due to the fact that God will not create us a bride to meet all of our needs, but we must search diligently for ourselves.

Genesis 2:22 "And the rib, which the Lord God had taken from man, made he woman, and brought her unto him."

Genesis 2:23 "And Adam said, This is now bone of my bones, and flesh of my flesh: she shall be called Woman, because she was taken out of Man."

From the beginning, Adam accepted the woman as being a part of him. When a man takes a wife, he must first see that woman as a part of him that is to be loved and cherished as himself just as Adam did. Some will see the money, house, cars, and other materialistic things of value rather than the person they marry. If you choose to marry someone and see anything other than the person you wouldn't mind being a part of, you have failed from the start. All material things may have great value initially, but over the years, they begin to depreciate. If a marriage is built upon material things, it will become meaningless. God forbid you lose those things which the marriage is built upon; you will also lose the marriage. A marriage is only as great as what you see in the other person and that person's value must be above anything you possess.

Every man should know when he meets a woman if that woman is suitable for him. Many relationships don't last because we select someone that is available rather than waiting on the individual that is most suitable. For the most suitable person may take the longest time to find, but waiting will be worth it in the end. The right person will be with you for a lifetime. Marriage can be a very unhappy part of your life with the wrong person. It is said that, **"There is no greater loss than choosing the wrong mate."**

To marry is a great responsibility on behalf of the man and the woman. For two people to successfully function together as a unit, God's plan has to be put to work. You must believe you can have a close relationship between you and your mate, as Adam stated, "Bone of my bones and flesh of my flesh." If someone is a part of you, you are more likely to give the same care to him or her as you would give to yourself. You must know in your heart that this person deserves to share everything you are about and everything you possess.

Love not one another in talk but in action and in honesty. For some with their mouth show much love, but their heart goes after their wants. In a marriage, you must love the other as yourself. Just because a couple gets married doesn't assure love. It can only be proven by giving to the other person. You can't love someone and not be willing to give your all.

When I make mistakes or make bad decisions, I don't look down on myself. I just correct them and move on. When the other person in the relationship makes the mistakes, we must be willing to accept their mistakes and move on.

Let's take a deeper look at the mistakes of our spouses. You have to understand that being married, you are one. When one or the other makes a mistake and you make a big deal about the details thereof, you begin to hinder yourself. Anything that affects the one also affects the other. So if you are going to waste time debating about who's right or who's wrong, you are really arguing against yourself because you are one. Just make a decision on the matter and move on.

God's ideal plan for true marital happiness is laid out in a **three-step process:**

Step 1—Leaving:

We must start with the man as God did. Man must forsake his father and mother first. Upon forsaking his father and mother, he must go out and establish a place in which he will live. If you cannot leave your parents and setup a place for yourself and your family, you are not ready for God's plan. Because leaving and setting up your own place will initiate the start of your role as a leader.

When the woman establishes the home, the plan of God will not work. While she is working and providing for the man, she is at the same time prohibiting him from fulfilling his purpose. God created the woman to be taken care of, and shame on you as a woman for operating outside the will of God. I am not here to command you to do anything. It is your decision to do as you please, but don't put the blame on anyone if you are not a *winner* in your relationship.

Step 2—Cleaving:

Looking back in chapter two, God created a place for Adam before the woman was presented to him. He is the same God yesterday, today, and forevermore. God did not say to the woman, "Leave your father and mother." Because when a woman resides with her parents prior to marriage, it is a safe haven for her. This is the ideal arrangement until a man wise enough and strong enough is willing and able to give her the same kind of love and protection she received from her father and mother.

Psalm 45:10 "Hearken, O daughter, and consider, and incline thine ear; forget also thine own people, and thy father's house;"

Psalm 45:11 "So shall the king greatly desire thy beauty: for he is thy Lord; and worship thou him."

When a man leaves and starts a new home, the woman comes to him. Therefore, he cleaves to his wife, giving her assurance that he will provide for her. As a woman, when you decide to go under the leadership of your husband, you must know that you are giving up total control of your freedom to do as you please. It is now entrusted in the hands of another human being, and you must know that he will do you good and not harm all the days of your life.

If a man does not leave completely, it will be almost impossible for him to cleave to his wife. When there is a lingering parental link, it can sometimes complicate a marriage. This may bring about long-term damage with circumstances which tend to be unforgivable to some.

Step 3—Becoming One:

A man and a woman must both be supportive of each other in all aspects of their relationship if it is to succeed. When they think as one, this causes them to become one flesh having completely united in life's purpose and pleasure. Even when they are apart from one another, they will always make decisions in the best interest of the other.

Genesis 2:24 "Therefore shall a man leave his father and mother, and shall cleave unto his wife: and they shall be one flesh."

The three-step plan for a successful marriage is simple but one step will not work without the others. In order to become one, you must cleave, and in order to cleave, you must leave. Have you ever tried riding a three-wheel bicycle with one of the wheels missing? If not, I would advise you not to do so because no matter which wheel it is, it will be extremely difficult to ride.

God created man with all the qualities required to manage a household. When there are decisions to be made, the man should always have the final say. If someone is out to destroy your home, the devil will most likely try to attack the woman first. Satan learned in the *Garden of Eden* that in order for him to get to the man, who's in control, he had to go through the weaker of the two, the woman.

When God wants answers, He always seeks out man. The enemy will always seek out the weaker one. When Adam and Eve took of the fruit thereof and did eat, their eyes were opened. They realized they were naked, and they heard the voice of the Lord God walking in the cool of the day. Adam and his wife hid themselves from the presence of God. He did not say "Adam and Eve, where art thou?" He called unto Adam only saying, "Where art thou?" God wants the man to always be responsible for what goes on in his house. God will hold the man accountable for the actions of his household. It will eliminate finger-pointing and blame-shifting.

Adam had direct orders from God what to do and what not to do. He told Adam, "You are free to eat from every tree in the garden with my blessing." There was only one tree God instructed him not to eat of, and he was told that the day he ate of that tree, he would surely die.

Genesis 2:16 "And the Lord God commanded the man, saying, Of every tree of the garden thou mayest freely eat:"

Genesis 2:17 "But of the tree of the knowledge of good and evil, thou shalt not eat of it: for in the day that thou eatest thereof thou shalt surely die."

Adam had a beautiful home, a wife created by God, and power and dominion over the fish of the sea, the fowl of the air and every living thing that moved upon the earth. What more can a man ask for than the inheritance of the earth?

Take notice in the world today, when a man appears to be doing well, you will find people trying everything to destroy him for no reason at all. It really doesn't matter who you are, there will always be someone standing in the shadows waiting for you to fall. The marriage structure that God gave will prevent many pitfalls. God's master plan for marriage works to perfection. When the man gives up his headship, you can expect any and just about everything to go wrong within the relationship.

Genesis 3:1 "Now the serpent was more subtile than any beast of the field which the Lord God had made. And he said unto the woman, Yea, hath God said, Ye shall not eat of every tree of the garden?"

Genesis 3:2 "And the woman said unto the serpent, We may eat of the fruit of the trees of the garden."

Genesis 3:3 "But of the fruit of the tree which is in the midst of the garden, God hath said, Ye shall not eat of it, neither shall ye touch it, lest ye die."

Genesis 3:4 "And the serpent said unto the woman, Ye shall not surely die:"

Genesis 3:5 "For God doth know that in the day ye eat thereof, then your eyes shall be opened, and ye shall be as gods, Knowing good and evil."

Genesis 3:6 "And when the woman saw that the tree was good for food, and that it was pleasant to the eyes, and a tree to be desired to make one wise, she took of the fruit thereof, and did eat, and gave also unto her husband with her; and he did eat."

It is very important that a man takes care of his house and those in it. When things go wrong, it should not be an argument because the responsibility rests in the man's hands. When the husband and wife are making decisions, it becomes easy to shift the blame on the other person, so no one takes the responsibility for the confusion.

The woman's submission to the man allows him to reach his greatest potential and make sound decisions. In return, he will look after her well-being as head of the household. She has a need for nothing because God blessed the man to be a strong provider against the odds.

Genesis 3:12 "And the man said, The woman whom thou gavest to be with me, she gave me of the tree, and I did eat."

Genesis 3:13 "And the Lord God said unto the woman, What is this that thou has done? And the woman said, The serpent beguiled me, and I did eat."

If a man today does not get the job done, it leaves a window of opportunity for the woman to take on added responsibility. The refusal of a man and woman to take on the roles which God has given them brings on a reversal of their marital roles, making life together almost unbearable. Take notice of what happened to Adam when he listened to Eve and ate of the fruit.

Many women today may think having a man as head of the house limits opportunities in life, but that's not true. If the wife is a true help to her husband, there is nothing he wouldn't do for her. Every man wants to feel like a complete man, and the only being that can give him that feeling is the woman. No man, animal, or hobby can make him whole other than the woman.

Genesis 3:16 "Unto the woman he said, I will greatly multiply thy sorrow and thy conception; in sorrow thou shalt bring forth children; and thy desire shall be to thy husband, and he shall rule over thee."

Genesis 3:17 "And unto Adam he said, Because thou has hearkened unto the voice of thy wife, and has eaten of the tree, of which I commanded thee, saying, Thou shalt not eat of it: cursed is the ground for thy sake; in sorrow shalt thou eat of it all the days of thy life."

Genesis 3:19 "In the sweat of thy face shalt thou eat bread, till thou return unto the ground; for out of it wast thou taken: for dust thou art, and unto dust shalt thou return."

It is imperative that a man work; it is the will of God. Look at many men today; some of them are with some woman without understanding who's trying to overpower the will of God. Due to reversal of the roles, many husbands depend on their wives to the point that some are one step from wearing a dress. Men, these things ought not to be. The woman was not made to rule over the man but to take care of him. She doesn't have the ability or strength to carry him and shouldn't be pressured to do so.

If the husband is not the head of the wife, is Christ therefore not the head of the church? If the wife is not subject unto her husband, is the church not subject to Christ? Many will disbelieve the fact that the man was instructed by God to rule over the woman. It is a disgrace before God that a woman will take a chance to rule over her husband. There are individuals sitting in churches all over the country who have taken a position of supremacy over the man, even after knowing what the word of God has to say.

The Lord gave Adam authority to name all of the living creatures. By naming the creatures, Adam demonstrated his dominion over them.

Genesis 2:19 *"And out of the ground, the Lord God formed every beast of the field, and every fowl of the air; and brought them unto Adam to see what he would call them: and whatsoever Adam called every living creature, that was the name thereof."*

Adam called his wife Eve. Naming his wife further reinforces his leadership and authority over her.

Genesis 3:20 *"And Adam called his wife's name Eve; because she was the mother of all living."*

At this point, I cannot express myself enough concerning the order of the husband and wife. God set the guide in the beginning with a few simple steps to follow. Right now, you may be a long way from being a *winner,* but if you follow the three steps, at least you will be heading in the right direction. One of the worst things to do is make the statement, "I don't know where I'm going, but I'm sure making good time." I want you to know where you are going and know how to make good time getting there.

Today, marriages have so many small circumstances that can bring about the end of a relationship. Just imagine a marriage after years where the husband and wife both work and believe in being equal in responsibilities or meeting halfway in household obligations. When one or the other is wrong about something or anything at all, who will be the first to forgive? It could be something as simple as taking out the trash. When all things are equal, who will take care of the little things in the marriage that are extremely necessary in order to make it functional? In some cases, forgetting to feed the wife or husband's pet will be grounds for a divorce.

Think for a moment, you build a home, a business, and give all you can, but it still never seems to be enough. This is because nothing works when all things are equal. Not everyone has the role of a boss at your place of employment. The boss has to be responsible for all of his or her employees and the work they produce; therefore, greater accountability comes with the position. Just as in the church, not everyone has the role of the pastor, for his followers entrust him with their lives. Now, why would anyone feel it takes two leaders to manage a household? Ask yourself, why is it that when you have a same-sex marriage, one individual will always play the masculine role and the other will play the feminine role? One wants to rule and the other wants to submit. Do you understand the point I am trying to make?

The Lord created His plan for the man and woman. Why not receive it with joy as you do with everything else? For example, as you receive it when the sun comes up after a good night's rest, like a rain pour after a drought or the beauty of nature when the seasons change. God created the heavens and the earth and saw that it was good and we appreciate His goodness every day.

God put man and woman in their order and saw that it was good. Priority in creation also validates man's authority over the woman. God could have created the woman first or both at the same time but this was not so. It was always His intention for the man to lead and the woman to follow.

I Corinthians 11:3 "But I would have you to know, that the head of every man is Christ; and the head of the woman is the man; and the head of Christ is God."

I Corinthians 11:8 "For the man is not of the woman; but the woman of the man."

I Corinthians 11:9 "Neither was the man created for the woman, but the woman for the man."

As a man, I can never think that I am better than the woman because she was created for a purpose. I will always respect the work of God. He gave the man special abilities that a woman will never be able to measure up to, and He created the woman with qualities that a man will never achieve or comprehend. God made it this way so we would need each other. *(God is truly wonderful.)* The key is, when you are trying to find your place, in all things get understanding.

I Peter 3:7 "Likewise, ye husbands, dwell with them according to knowledge, giving honor unto the wife, as unto the weaker vessel, and as being heirs together of the grace of life; that your prayers be not hindered."

To all that have their sights on becoming a *winner*, you must follow God's rules just as you follow the rules or instructions for anything else. The husband is strong yet he needs someone to take care of him. The wife, on the other hand, is weaker and needs her husband to protect her. Together, I hope you can begin to see that God's plan can make you a *winner*.

I cannot speak for anyone else, but I speak freely for myself. Some will get the impression that I am a male chauvinist. If that is the way I appear unto you, don't blame me, get mad at God. I truly love who I am and the position God has put me in. I love being a man and will never complain about the work or responsibilities God has laid upon me. God instructed me to take care of the woman in every aspect of life, and I will be a man and accept my position always holding it with honor all the days of my life.

As a woman, I believe you would be following God's plan if you did not work on someone's job. Your position in life is more important than working a nine-to-five shift. **Let no one reduce your value to a paycheck.** The plan which God has for you is far greater than what meets the eye.

Let's take a look at some of the ways in which you can help improve our society. If you are married or getting married, stay at home and be a helper to your husband. Raise your children; don't leave it for others to do what God intended for you to do. The home that your husband has provided for you, take care of it. You would be amazed at the effect it will have on your household and those within it.

The country as a whole is falling apart due to the overwhelming demand of the woman having to go out and provide for her family. Many of the young men and women sitting in jail today are results of the father not working and the mother working, not having time to be at home. Leaving children in the care of someone who doesn't have the same love of the family makes all the difference. Although there have been many children that have grown up and become successful in life, I feel that all children should have the same opportunity. But, their chances are greater being in the mother's care until they reach the age of eighteen.

Most single mothers with kids are doing a wonderful job taking care of their household alone, but that's not the way to add years to their lives. I do give the woman respect for trying. You can take a volleyball and put it in a hard-fought match, game after game. The ball will always hold up because it was designed for that purpose. Take that same ball and use it in a basketball game, and it will not make it through the first quarter of play because it will lose its composure due to the constant pounding on a hard surface. The woman is strong, but she was not designed to handle extreme pressure.

You must not forget that the Lord God did not take the man and the woman and put them in the garden to dress and keep it. God put the man to work, taking care of the garden alone.

Regardless of what we accomplish in life, we will never change what was set in motion from the beginning of time.

Chapter 5
Let The Search Begin
(The Dating Phase)

Being a winner is all about how well you prepare yourself. I know some of you could not wait to get to this chapter, but if you have not read chapters one through four, the instructions in this chapter will be hard to understand and execute. You will have no idea of what to look for in a person during the intense selection process. So before you proceed any further, go back to the beginning of the book and obtain the necessary blueprint for becoming a winner. Now that you've done so, let the search begin.

You must understand that God will no longer take a rib from man and make a woman suitable for him. Instead, God has entrusted you with the obligation of finding someone that's right for you. Therefore, whether you select a fool or wise individual, you are ultimately responsible for the selection you've made. I've heard the statement, "God gave him to me" or "God gave her to me." This is false; God put an end to that when Adam blamed Him in the beginning when Adam made his first mistake.

Adam blamed the woman and God, since God was the one who brought her to him. If Adam selected Eve, who would he blame then? Whom you select is totally up to you, good or bad.

Selecting someone is a great responsibility and should be considered a serious process that is not to be taken lightly. Take your time in looking for the right person. Many times, people tend to think something is wrong with you when you are single. They may even make an attempt to find someone for you. Don't allow anyone to put pressure on you to select a mate. Thoughts under pressure can lead to you choosing someone for all the wrong reasons. Just because an individual is available doesn't mean they are necessarily suitable. A wrong pick can lead to many sad days and sleepless nights. There are people in graves, prison, and mental institutions for making a bad judgment during their search. You can be blinded by the thought that you know a person inside and out, but that reality is nonexistent. With blindness as such, you will not accept counsel from anyone who could possibly prevent you from making a terrible mistake. On many occasions, couples inform me of how well they know one another, but most of the time, it turned out to be untrue. The majority who make such a statement tend to encounter problems in the marriage from the beginning.

Jeremiah 17:9 "The heart is deceitful above all things, and desperately wicked: who can know it?"

Before trying to find the individual who is right for you, you must first examine yourself. You need to know your strengths and weaknesses. When you've identified them, whatever area you are lacking in, the person you select must be able to make up the difference. Ask yourself, what can I bring to this relationship? If you aren't bringing anything to the table, why should you expect any more from the other person? "Don't expect more out of a person than you are willing to give yourself."

It is very important to have a well-balanced relationship where both individuals complement each other. If a person comes along and you truly don't feel they are the one, have the courage to walk away. There is nothing worse than when a sprinter is preparing for the 100 meter with shoes one size to small. That person knows before the race gets started that they have no chance to win. Just as in a relationship, you cannot start out with low expectations and expect to be a winner in the end. A person who doesn't fit or measure up can't improve you as a person but can limit you in your accomplishments.

The search is supposed to lead to a marriage that is meant to last a lifetime, but it will quickly fall apart if you have different spiritual values, goals, and aspirations. Therefore, the road to get there must be well traveled, eliminating any detours or "short cuts." The race is not to the swift but to the one that endures. As in anything, you have to start out like you can hold out. The journey is a lifelong expectancy and you need to know if the other person is capable of going the distance and withstanding the test of time. I believe that a plane burns the greatest amount of fuel leaving the ground, so don't be in a rush.

You must put in a lot of effort making things right. There is nothing worse than a bad relationship.

A relationship that has failed is one of the worst investments you can make. Forget about a thirty-year mortgage or a six-year car note, it is the relationship that can bring about the most detrimental issues of life. It is better to be patient and invest the time in order to make certain you have the right person before taking flight in a marriage. Approach it with caution rather than going full speed ahead into something that could have a negative affect on you the rest of your life.

Proverbs 18:22 "Whoso findeth a wife findeth a good thing, and obtaineth favor of the Lord."

Finding a wife or a husband is not as simple as going to the grocery store and picking up a loaf of bread from the shelf. Some make it seem as if a good man or a good woman can be found on any street corner for a dime a dozen. This is an incorrect assumption from Solomon's prospective. Solomon was blessed with wisdom and understanding, he had this to say:

Ecclesiastes 7:27 "Behold, this have I found, saith the preacher, counting one by one, to find out the account:"

Ecclesiastes 7:28 "Which yet my soul seeketh, but I find not: one man among a thousand have I found; but a woman among all those have I not found."

Ecclesiastes 7:29 "Lo, this only have I found, that God hath made man upright; but they have sought out many inventions."

Solomon was the wisest man who ever lived, but with all of his wisdom, even he did not understand all of the mysteries of a man and a woman. With all of the power, honor, and wealth he possessed, he could not follow the almighty God due to his wives seeking other gods. As Solomon states, "God has made us upright and given us a plan, but we have sought out different schemes trying to establish things our way. There is only one way and that is the plan of God."

The Bible gives us a good example of how difficult it is to find that perfect mate. Solomon had his mind set on pleasing God. Out of a thousand women, he could not find one that encouraged him to keep looking to his God. Just as in Solomon's story, having the wrong companion can cause you to turn your back on God and anything else of importance.

I Kings 11:1 "But King Solomon loved many strange women, together with the daughter of Pharaoh, women of the Moabites, Ammonites, Edomites, Zidonians, and Hittites;"

I Kings 11:2 "Of the nations concerning which the Lord said unto the children of Israel, Ye shall not go in to them, neither shall they come in unto you: for surely they will turn away your heart after their gods: Solomon clave unto these in love."

I Kings 11:3 "And he had seven hundred wives, princesses, and three hundred concubines: and his wives turned away his heart."

I Kings 11:4 "For it came to pass, when Solomon was old, that his wives turned away his heart after other gods: and his heart was not perfect with the lord his God, as was the heart of David his father."

When you are in search for that special someone, make sure you have a plan of your own. Be sure to list what you expect from the other person and the expectations you have for yourself. Before a special dinner is prepared by a chef, the first step is to make a list of the ingredients needed to complete the dinner planned. He will allow no one to add or delete from it because he knows exactly what he needs. He goes to the store, gets the ingredients required, and prepares the meal to his liking. Just as the chef, if you don't establish a plan for your life, someone will automatically include you in their plan or create a plan for you. This will leave you with no control of your destination.

Don't seek someone just because they have certain qualities about them, but make sure you find them to be necessary. Don't just say you love them, you must also say that you need them. I have seen so many couples having the time of their lives while dating. They take trips together, wine and dine one another, and go for walks in the park. Some walk hand in hand as if they were joined at the hip during birth. Then after they decide to get married, all the fun is gone. This is due to the fact that they didn't take the time to resolve their differences during the dating phase. Instead, they focused on the enjoyment and pleasure.

Dating should be one of the most serious phases you experience in your life. Many times, the success or failure of a marriage is determined by what you negotiate during the dating process. Don't be afraid to ask questions or voice your concerns. Think about this for a moment: If I decide to take a trip in a car from Florida to Tennessee, the first thing I need to know is whether or not the vehicle I'm driving is capable of making the trip. The motor has to be functioning properly, the tires in good condition, and the gas tank full. If there are any problems, I will correct them before getting on the road. I have to be serious about the car going the distance in order to avoid a hazardous situation. When I know the car is in good working order, I can begin my journey with a clear conscience and have fun all the way to my destination.

The point I'm trying to make is that you should be uncompromising when dating so you can experience enjoyment during your years of marriage. Some have neglected the importance of being serious during the dating phase by having lots of fun, resulting in them being miserable in the marriage. You can always tell if a person is right or wrong for you. Don't overlook the signs or red flags. Sometimes, we don't want to accept the truth that we are with someone who looks nice on the outside but is full of hell on the inside. The person who's right for you may not be extremely attractive or extremely educated, but they are willing to give you the best they have. A person who is physically appealing and well educated hasn't always proved to be the best selection in my book.

If you are one of those dating for the fun of being with someone, it would be wise to make it clear upfront before anything takes place. Being honest is a good way to start out; there is no harm to either person at this point. To find two individuals who interpret the meaning of their relationship the same way is extremely rare. To one, it may appear they are the one but to the other person, it may only be a game or something done out of convenience and not because they care for that person.

Again, be patient, the right person will one day come into the picture. Don't focus on who has who. You are created special, and no one has an edge in the search. Regardless of the qualities others possess, you have the same right to be happy with the person you select in due time.

Ecclesiastes 9:11 *"I returned and saw under the sun, that the race is not to the swift, nor the battle to the strong, neither yet bread to the wise, nor yet riches to men of understanding, nor yet favor to the men of skill; but time and chance happeneth to them all."*

Allow me to share a little humor with you. A young lady came to me and said she was having a problem finding someone to be with.

She said, "I have been praying constantly to no avail."

I responded by saying, "What type of individual are you looking for?"

She told me, "I am in search of a husband."

Within seconds, I told her that she was looking for the wrong man. Her search should have really been directed to finding a man because a husband is someone who's married and already taken.

It is amazing to see people taking a chance in life with someone with no future plans concerning marriage. If the person is not ready for marriage, you should still be able to tell if they are qualified to be a wife or husband. No one ever said you have to rush into marriage, but it is clear to me that you can't receive the same care and respect from a person when they are not willing to make a commitment.

I must address the issues of submitting before you say *I DO* at the altar. Not having made the trip to the altar, why as a single and free person will you allow someone to control your life in everything you do as if you are married. According to the Bible, you must obey your parents until you get married, but many will listen to the person they're seeing rather than their parents. If a man wants that type of control over you or he wants you to submit, tell him to marry you. You benefit nothing by obeying the person you're with, but there are great rewards for obeying your parents. Until a woman marries, she should be subject to her father and after marriage to her husband.

Ephesians 6:1 "Children obey your parents in the Lord: for this is right."

Ephesians 6:2 "HONOR THY FATHER AND MOTHER; which is the first commandment with promise;"

Ephesians 6:3 "THAT IT MAY BE WELL WITH THEE, AND THOU MAYEST LIVE LONG ON THE EARTH."

The above verse is not telling you to obey only Christian parents but also non-Christian parents. Basically, any instruction that is in line with God's will should be obeyed. When someone obeys or disobeys their parents, that should be a measuring stick for the other person. One of the things you should pay close attention to is how well he or she respects his or her father and mother. Don't be fooled into thinking it's not like that with you because you think they care for you more. Those parents loved and cared for that individual from birth until you came into their life. Think for a moment, you may be beautiful or handsome, but there is no way you can erase what the parents of that person have done for them and given to them. If you see disrespect shown toward the parents, that should give you a very good indication of what you will be dealing with.

A woman must be very watchful and sober-minded when searching for ***Mr. Right***. During the search is where the woman must stand strong, because when she marries, she no longer has the right to demand what she wants. The man you desire must be able to provide for you and protect you in all areas of life. Is he quick to hit you? If yes, it will not last. Some people think this type of behavior is a symbol of love. Maybe someone talked you into thinking that way or maybe it happened to a family member. Regardless of the source, it is wrong to hit on a woman.

Once physical abuse enters a relationship, it takes on a mind of its own and can spin out of control before anyone realizes it. Some people have killed their mate or spouse but really loved them. The first sign of physical aggression displayed should be stopped immediately. The refusal to put an end to this type of behavior will result in it becoming an ongoing habit. People have drinking and/or smoking addictions, and there are also some who have a hitting disorder. Be certain to avoid a situation such as this because no good can come from it.

Next, can you trust him? If no, it will not last. If you decide to marry this individual, how can he rule over you and possibly children? All that you have and own must be put in his care one day if you decide to marry him. You must totally believe that he will do you good and not evil every day of your life.

Is he working? Or did he at least have a job when you met him? If the answer is no, then don't get ahead of yourself. Having a job for a man is the number one priority defining his leadership. Once a woman accepts a man's excuse for not having a job, he will use an excuse later in the marriage when you need him the most. God told man he had to work.

And God said unto Adam, "In the sweat of your face, you shalt eat bread, until you return unto the ground. This was man's punishment, to work all the days of his life."

If you feel it's okay for a man not to work, shame on you for giving him a free ride. You allow him to have too much available time and idle hands are the "*devil's workshop.*"

II Thessalonians 3:10 "For even when we were with you, this we commanded you, that if any would not work, neither should he eat."

I Timothy 5:8 "But if any provide not for his own, and specially for those of his own house, he hath denied the faith, and is worse than an infidel."

The Bible states that for a man not to work is morally worse than a person that doesn't believe in God. An individual may not have all the requirements it takes to manage a household at the moment, but they do show some promising signs that they are capable of doing so. The woman's responsibilities will be too great after marriage to worry about the finances in the household. The issues and excuses will not disappear when you receive your marriage papers. For some unknown reason, some ladies will allow a man to lie around doing nothing while she works all day. Remember, whatever you allow, God will allow because He has given us sound instructions.

During the dating period, each person must learn about the other's dreams, visions, and purpose. Dreams must not be overshadowed by personalities or appearance. The dreams and visions are what drive us to keep going in life.

Proverbs 29:18 "Where there is no vision the people perish: but he that keepeth the law, happy is he."

Make sure that the other person is willing to allow you to pursue your goals with or without their involvement. They may not see what you are trying to achieve, but they're willing to support you to the end. There are many people today who are suffering due to a lack of communication during the courtship. The ideal couple before the marriage has become a ticking time bomb during the marriage because they were too busy looking and touching prior to marriage, whereas the listening factor never came into the picture.

The potential of many has been wasted because of two different agendas within the relationship. Believe me when I speak about this, it brings tears to my eyes. I had a front row seat in a case such as this. My oldest brother, whom I love very dearly, was an all-around athlete from grade school throughout high school. He was the young man I admired and patterned myself after while growing up. Not only was he good in sports but also had the look that turned heads wherever he went. He was in the newspaper on a regular basis, and I took it upon myself to get a copy every time. I was extremely proud to be his brother.

During his senior year, he received letters from colleges all over the nation for his overwhelming abilities on the football field. He had not made a decision as to which college he would attend as there were several to choose from. Before graduation, he started to date a beautiful young lady. She had the appearance but not the same goals in life. In other words, they weren't heading in the same direction. His goal was to play in college and hopefully get drafted to play in the

NFL. Her goal was to marry him so she could have a man next to her. One month after they graduated, the marriage took place, and instantly, he lost sight of his goals and vision. Soon after, the drinking and partying started. Before he came to himself, the opportunities he wanted had passed.

They had no plans or goals in the marriage, so it ended in a bitter divorce. Thinking about what he lost was very hard for him to take. Drinking became his escape route. He has been drinking daily for the past thirty-two years. Every time he sobers up, what he lost comes to mind, and then he starts to cry. In his mind, the drinking must continue in order to chase away the thoughts of "what if." As for me, I love my brother more now than I ever did. Despite the state he is currently in and the circumstances that plague him daily, he will always be a star in my eyes.

I think it is better to stay single even if you feel you have what it takes to be a good mate. One can deal with being single, but being in a bad relationship is much worse.

Proverbs 24:6 "For by wise counsel thou shalt make thy war: and in multitude of counsellors there is safety."

There are so many different circumstances that can keep two people from functioning as a complete unit that will withstand the storms of life.

I have found that bringing a child or children from a previous relationship into a new relationship is one of the most difficult situations for the other to overcome. Not because the other person doesn't like kids but due to the problems that will come along with the child or children. This is one of the areas during the search that should be of great concern. Not only will you deal with the person you have chosen but you will also deal with the child's other parent.

While raising your child as a single parent, it will appear as if the mother or father of the child has disappeared. Then, as soon as you get involved with someone else, they reappear. Once they appear, he or she wants a say in what goes on with the child. For me, this is where it should stop. The rules must be laid down and strictly enforced.

You can be a good woman or a good man in the relationship, but when there are children involved, the outside influences will play a major role in what you do and how you do it. You may be able to control what goes on between you and your mate, but it is impossible to do so when it comes to the actions of the outside person. That other parent can wreak havoc on the relationship at anytime. It has been revealed time and time again that most problems seem to arise when things are going well. As long as both individuals are happy with their situation, they are more than willing to work together for the sake of peace. But if, on the other hand, one is miserable, they want everyone else they're associated with to be miserable also, because misery loves company.

There was a couple across from my house who had recently moved in. Every time I saw them, they appeared to be getting along wonderfully. I had no knowledge that a child was included in the equation. Early one morning, I was on my way to work when I noticed a car across from me pull up and stop. The woman got out with a baby, knocked on the couple's door, put the baby down on the doorstep, and drove off. The man came out, picked the child up, and went back inside. Regardless of what he and the woman living with him had planned, it was interrupted by *that outside influence.* Now, they must rethink their future plans.

You can have several different scenarios, but many times, the results are the same. Stress on the relationship can lead to a disaster with very few survivors. Only the strong can survive, and in order for you to gain the strength needed, you must be serious about your courtship. It's all a part of being a *winner.*

I will give you another situation that I recall taking place. There was this gentleman who was an excellent man who did all the right things before and during his marriage. He dated then married this lady with three children from two different men. Neither guy wanted to be with her and the children. The husband went out and purchased a home for them and worked six days a week providing for his household. She had no need to work because he took on all the responsibilities by himself.

Everything was perfect, he thought, until it was time to discipline the kids. There were no beatings, only simple punishments such as no allowance or no television after school. When the parents were not around, they each called their fathers and told them of the punishment. The very next day, the husband received a phone call from one of the children's fathers criticizing him for his child's punishment. After a while, the wife started to change, and the kids became distant which later caused the marriage to fall apart.

The discussion of how a child can affect the relationship is one of the most overlooked topics during the stages of dating. Just because the situation regarding the children was ignored doesn't mean it will go away. If anything, it will make you wish you had spent more time working out the details prior to it spinning out of control.

Take this simple advice when dealing with children because they can get caught in the middle while you are busy kissing and hugging. What's really important is the welfare and mental state of the children. Individuals lose sight of this as they feel catering to the man or woman they are with takes precedence over caring for the child or children. You should never, under any circumstances, put a man or woman before your child during the search. When kids are involved, it is very important to seek counseling, but be sure it is from a wise man.

Proverbs 20:5 "Counsel in the heart of man is like deep water; but a man of understanding will draw it out."

To the woman, if you went out and established your own place, do not allow the man to move in. Even if he did not purchase a thing within your home, he will still want to control it. It's man's nature to take charge over a woman. Do not play the wife role prior to marriage, because it will not benefit you later if you decide to marry him.

In today's society, the single people are having a ton of fun which tends to overpower the important things in life. Some will marry and end up feeling like the only thing going on in their relationship is what to do and what not to do. Due to the lack of understanding in some marriages, not many can convince someone else how good marriage is.

A woman should evaluate herself before getting involved in a relationship and again before marriage. She must not depend on a man unless he volunteers to help her out. If he doesn't, that will further enlighten you about what kind of person you are with. Believe me, if a man cares, he will always look out for you even while you're dating. No matter what, a good man will always be a good man in everything he does.

If a single woman is working, she should be excited to know that one day she will get married and not have to work. Her thoughts should shift to improving her household, taking care of her husband, the home, and possibly her children. If you are a single woman currently working, taking care of a man, children, and a home, what type of joy could you possibly receive if you were to get married today?

After taking a hard look at the challenge of the search, it should be a wonderful and exciting time in your life. You get the opportunity to select the person of your dreams. Take your time; the right person is somewhere for you. Look at things this way, finding the right person will be quicker than you think because now you are looking for them and they are looking for you. Don't settle for second place; it's not as much fun as being a *winner.*

When you find someone during your search, make sure he or she has everything you are looking for in a relationship. Remember, you can't change anyone; what you see is what you get. ***Ask the Lord to direct your heart and feelings. Many blessings and enjoyment as you search.***

Chapter 6
Marriage

How sweet it is to be married with the knowledge of God. He has given us the perfect plan essential to making us winners in our relationships. Everything you've read up to this point will play an important role in your relationship. If you've reached this chapter, the search is over and you should have married the person most suitable to complete you in every phase of your life. According to the Bible, two have become one, creating the greatest duo on the face of this earth. You've waited patiently for the right person and now it's time to experience growth, success, fun, and excitement. So buckle up and enjoy being married because you deserve to be happy.

When you find the right person, everything about you will get better. God intended for both individuals within the marriage to be happy. He created the perfect combination when He created the man and woman. The two are better than one because they will have a good return. They can double their strength and help each other overcome many obstacles in life. One plus one equals two not zero. Do the math! Adding someone to your life should make it better or change it for the better. Everything that was going on in your life as a single person must improve when you get married. Just imagine putting two engines in an automobile. You will definitely expect greater performance out of the vehicle with two engines over the vehicle with only one engine, right? If you are not getting the performance you desire, disappointment will soon follow. I'm sure you've heard the saying "I can do bad by myself." Maybe you have made that statement, also.

If you are married, take a moment to examine yourself. Are you better as a person now or before you got married? Let's say before you got married, you owned a car. Now that you're married, do you have two cars, a better car, or no car at all? Let's say you had your own place before marriage. Now that you're married, did your living arrangements become better or did you and the family move in with your parents, your spouse's parents, or a friend?

Ecclesiastes 4:9 "Two are better than one; because they have a good reward for their labor."

Ecclesiastes 4:10 "For if they fall, the one will lift up his fellow: but woe to him that is alone when he falleth; for he hath not another to help him up."

Ecclesiastes 4:11 "Again, if two lie together, then they have heat: but how can one warm alone?"

Ecclesiastes 4:12 "And if one prevail against him, two shall withstand him; and a threefold cord is not quickly broken."

Marriage is the greatest institution there is. You must be willing to share your total life with someone without having a second thought. Total trust in one another is a must. It is important for you to believe in each other during the good and bad times. If you are not ready for this challenge, stay away from marriage. Believe me, you will have good times but the bad times will come also. When the bad times come, you must be willing to stick together as you did during the good times.

The Bible speaks about Job. He was a man who was upright and one who feared God. He had great wealth which made him the greatest of all the men of the east. Job was a righteous man in God's eyes, yet he went through some tough times due to no fault of his own. He lost his family and his wealth but even though he lost everything, Job never gave up trusting in God.

Job 1:21 "And said, Naked came I out of my mother's womb, and naked shall I return thither: the Lord gave, and the Lord hath taken away; blessed be the name of the Lord."

Job 1:22 "In all this Job sinned not, nor charged God foolishly."

At this point in Job's life, you would think that the hard times were over, but the trials continued. His health, which is life's most precious gift one can receive, was challenged also. In the midst of everything going wrong, Job held fast his integrity. He remained a perfect and upright man, one who feared God and shunned evil. I believe Job trusted in God and followed His plan completely. With so much taking place within his life, you must begin to wonder what stopped him from giving up.

During the course of Job's trials, his wife was not mentioned. Nevertheless, when all of their natural possessions were lost and all that remained was her husband, she then appeared. The first thing she questioned was his status as a man. Many marry based on what an individual may have and not the person. Job was still the man she married, but because he had lost everything, his wife suggested that he curse God just as the devil predicted.

There will be many who doubt your success in the marriage. Job's wife could not hold up to the pressures of life. That's why God made it clear in the beginning that the woman was to be a helper to man and not rule over him. God did not create her for that role.

Job 2:9 "Then said his wife unto him, Dost thou still retain thine integrity? curse God, and die."

Job 2:10 "But he said unto her, Thou speakest as one of the foolish women speaketh. What? shall we receive good at the hand of God, and shall not receive evil? In all of this did not Job sin with his lips."

Sometimes, when things go badly, you will find the husband or the wife more willing to walk away from the relationship. Many times, couples put their strength in material things rather than each other. A man's life does not consist of the things he has or does not have. God made man strong, therefore the husband must hold fast and keep believing that he can see his family through the toughest of times.

Job lost everything but he never gave up. After his struggles, Job went on to enjoy life and his latter end was more blessed than the beginning. Just as in Job's marriage, many marriages will experience hard times. Difficult circumstances are a part of the process. Don't be so willing to give up at the first sign of trouble. Trust in one another because that's when you will see if you both are truly compatible.

Once in the marriage, you should always respect the goals and wishes of one another if they are in line with what pleases God. No two people think alike. Everyone has an agenda or ideas, and sometimes even when we are wrong, we still hold on to the thought that we are right.

In a marriage, always look for the right way and not your way. Never get in to the mindset where you are constantly trying to prove the other one wrong. Every way to us is right in our own eyes and proving it will be a fight that could last a lifetime. God said there must be one leader in all things just as there is only one God. Having only one in control of the institution of marriage is no exception.

The husband is the head of the wife, and this is a divine appointment from God. The husband has the responsibility to protect and provide for the wife. He must also provide spiritual leadership within the household. The wife should submit to her husband in all areas of life and in every issue that may arise, those that she agrees with and those which she may not agree with. She must believe that her husband will make the right decision concerning what's best for the marriage.

Philippians 2:2 "Fulfill ye my joy, that ye be likeminded, having the same love, being of one accord, of one mind."

Philippians 2: 3 "Let nothing be done through strife or vainglory; but in lowliness of mind let each esteem other better than themselves."

Philippians 2:4 "Look not every man on his own things, but every man also on the things of others."

God wants the husband and wife to live in total harmony. He gives six key points to follow in the above scriptures: 1) having the same love, 2) being of one accord, 3) of one mind, 4) let nothing be done through strife or vainglory, 5) let each esteem other better than themselves and 6) look on the things of others.

Today, marriages are all about what the other person can do for them. Instead, marriage should be about having the right person and becoming a servant, friend, and companion to that person. Don't take the road many are taking within marriage. God's plan protects us even when we grow older because the love we give in the relationship will be returned when we are old and can't do for ourselves. He knows that there is no performance in the grave so you must experience enjoyment while on earth.

The Lord doesn't expect us to sit around and be miserable, but to live joyfully, eating, drinking, and so on together with the one we love. God clearly approves of the enjoyment of this life. His will is that we might have life and have it more abundantly.

A husband's love for his wife brings about her submission to him. He is to make sure all her needs are met to where she does not have to beg or plead for what she wants. A wife's submission to her husband must come from her own free will. The husband cannot force his wife to submit. If he tries, it will start to work against him.

Becoming a *winner* in your relationship requires you to take heed to the perfect plan from God. This plan was first created in the beginning when God formed man and woman. He knew then what it would take for a husband and wife to function together as one.

Genesis 2:24 "Therefore shall a man leave his father and mother, and shall cleave unto his wife: and they shall be one flesh."

The same plan holds true today. God is the same throughout all generations. We have been given the perfect guide for a marriage so both the husband and wife can be *winners* at the same time. Only the almighty God could have come up with such a master plan that can stand for generations. **JESUS** came and repeated the exact plan that was applied in the first marriage in the *Garden of Eden.* Every step that was given to Adam and his wife is for everyone today.

God's master plan for true marriage contentment doesn't allow for the husband and wife to compete against one another but for them to complete each other. The plan is simple to follow.

***Matthew 19:4** "And he answered and said unto them, Have you not read, that he which made them at the beginning MADE THEM MALE AND FEMALE,"*

***Matthew 19:5** "And said, For THIS CAUSE SHALL A MAN LEAVE HIS FATHER AND MOTHER, AND SHALL CLEAVE TO HIS WIFE: AND THEY TWAIN SHALL BE ONE FLESH?"*

***Matthew 19:6** "Wherefore they are no more twain, but one flesh. What therefore God hath joined together, let not man put asunder."*

The plan **JESUS gives** is laid out in a **three-step process** also:

Step 1—Leaving:

Once again, we must start with the man as God did with Adam. Man must forsake his father and mother. Upon forsaking his father and mother, he should go out and establish a place in which he will live. You must be willing to leave your parents and setup a place for yourself or your family. Leaving and creating your own place will prove your self-rule.

God did not intend for the woman to leave and create the home. If she sets up the home, it should only be for herself alone or with her children. If a woman goes into a relationship wrongly, she will most likely end up wrong. It is very difficult to correct a vehicle that is spinning out of control. If you cleave to a man before he leaves, you will be setting yourself up for disappointment.

Step 2—Cleaving:

God created a place for Adam before the woman was presented to him. God knows exactly what works best in the relationship. With God there is not even the slightest change; He is immutable. God did not say to the woman, "Leave your father and mother." God made man and woman and He was acquainted with everything about them. When the wife receives unconditional love from her husband, she will be willing to follow him wherever he goes.

Ruth 1:16 "And Ruth said, Entreat me not to leave thee, or to return from following after thee: for whither thou goest, I will go; and where thou lodgest, I will lodge: thy people shall be my people, and thy God my God:"

Ruth 1:17 "Where thou diest, will I die, and there will I be buried: the Lord do so to me, and more also, if aught but death part thee and me."

When a couple gets married, their new place of dwelling should already be established. The husband must cleave to his wife, giving her self-confidence that she made the right decision. The husband and wife should have unquenchable love that will not be diminished by circumstances.

When the husband and wife don't cleave to each other, they will fill the void with someone or something else. One or the other can easily cleave to the job, a friend, a parent, or any natural asset. In such circumstances, the marriage will fail. In the marriage, there is nothing more important than one another. If you are not willing to put your mate first, before anyone or anything other than *Christ*, marriage should not be the road you take.

Step 3—Becoming One:

A husband and a wife must always be helpful to each other when needed. They must be as one, totally united in every way possible. It could be as simple as going to the store; when one or the other buys something, they will always think of their companion. If their mate is not around, you can't tell because one will always speak on behalf of the other in a *good way.*

The three-step plan for a successful marriage is simple, but one step will not work without the others. Therefore, it's impossible to have one without the other, and be sure that leaving is not the only reason for getting married.

When all hell is breaking out around you, enjoy your husband or wife whom you love. If you cleave to one another you will never know that you are in the midst of a storm. Allow your husband or wife to be your strength in the time of trouble. After things settle down, you will have a newfound love for each other.

If you can't follow the plan of the almighty God who created the heavens and the earth, what makes you think someone else has a better way? Why would you complain about His plan for the perfect marriage when you don't complain about the beauty which He has created for you to behold daily?

A married couple has a better opportunity for a great marriage if they don't rely on their parents or others for financial support, emotional stability, or guidance. Sometimes couples cripple themselves from day one because they go into the relationship depending on outside support. If you start with your hands out, you will become dependent on whomever or whatever the source is. People will lead you to believe they are willing to help and then they give you just enough to fail. Make sure you are totally independent when the marriage starts.

When we are born, we do not have the ability to take care of ourselves. While growing up in life, we ask for help from our parents on a daily basis. Becoming an adult is not going to change our dependant way of thinking which we learned in the early stages of our life; learning how to depend on someone else comes naturally to us as human beings.

Many people think it's a high risk to step out on their own. Take a look around; it doesn't matter where you live, the results are the same all over our society. The average age for staying at home has increased dramatically in the last ten years. If it continues on this track, ten years from now, you won't know who is the father or son because they will look the same age.

JESUS encourages us to leave and stand on our own when we decide to marry someone. That is the only way we can go from being a follower to gaining independence. God knew that in the beginning, it will be a struggle, but don't listen to the sad stories of others causing fear to come over you. No two marriages will have the same circumstances, so don't allow anyone to tell you of their experiences.

I once heard that some scientists did a study on the bumble bee in a wind tunnel and discovered their wing span in comparison to their body size should prohibit them from flying. The bee, being ignorant of the finding, goes on to fly anyway. If you don't listen to the opinions and views about marriages from others, you may have an excellent chance of making your marriage work, as in the case of the bee.

The husband is and will always be the head of the house **period**! He can't change it by wearing a dress, growing long hair, or not working. The man is the head, and if he's in any other place, you will find yourself fighting against God. Many wives are wondering where they went wrong. They begin having thoughts like he doesn't love me anymore, he has someone else, he sleeps in the other room, he doesn't talk much anymore, and the list goes on. If you are having these thoughts, check to see if you have given him total control.

Just because the wife is working, it doesn't give her the right to rule. I don't care if her husband doesn't have a job. You favored him in the search and you knew what kind of man he was. "Little lady, just get out of the way and let him take his place." If you allow him to take his rightful place, you will start to see harmony within the house. There is no negotiation that can make the position God gave him disappear.

I Corinthians 11:3 "But I would have you know, that the head of every man is Christ; and the head of every woman is the man; and the head of the Christ is God."

I Corinthians 11:8 "For the man is not of the woman; but the woman of the man."

I Corinthians 11:9 "Neither was the man created for the woman; but the woman for the man."

This is the way God wants it to work. If you have a better way, prove to someone that you can create the heavens as God did. He has proven over and over that His words have power. God has given man responsibility and accountability not superiority over his wife. God created both the man and woman equal but gave them different functions and responsibilities.

Think on this for a moment: If you were hired in a restaurant to sweep the floor and you did a good job while doing so, the supervisor will turn and praise you. As a result, you receive a promotion and a raise. The next day, you go to work feeling good because you think you are good at what you do. You then get above yourself and go to the stove to prepare the meals for the customers. When the boss comes in, what do you think he's going to do, pat you on the back? I think not, you are getting fired. Not because you can't cook but because it's not your place or responsibility.

Romans 12:3 "For I say, through the grace given unto me, to every man that is among you, not to think of himself more highly than he ought to think; but to think soberly, according as God hath dealt to every man the measure of faith."

God has given the man and woman specific gifts to enable them to perform in the capacity in which He created them. God doesn't want the man to underestimate himself or the woman to overestimate herself. We all have a free will to do as we please, but don't let that free will hinder you from enjoying life.

When the husband falls short in taking care of his responsibilities within the marriage, it leaves an opening for the woman to take on added responsibility. As a result, the power of a man is decreased and his role in headship is less important. By chance the husband and wife don't live up to the roles which God has given them, the marriage can experience great hardship. This can ultimately cause a gap in the relationship. When such a gap exists, it is better to be single and alone than married and lonely.

A man who loves his wife will not be rude, unkind, or cruel toward her in any way. Actions such as name calling must be avoided as it can be extremely destructive. In some cases, the effects thereof will never be forgotten. Certain behavioral patterns tend to make it obvious that you can be married and not have love for the person you are married to. Just because someone agreed to be a part of a marriage doesn't necessarily mean they have love for the person they are marrying.

Having a husband as head of the house will not limit the wife's opportunities in life. If the wife truly is a support to her husband, he should be willing to do anything within his power for her. God did not create man and woman for the purpose of obtaining material things in life; they were created for each other. Today a man and woman are measured by their material possessions and not by their character. Sometimes when the natural things we possess are no longer there, the husband or wife isn't either. Job was a man who trusted in the Lord and he said, "The Lord gave and the Lord has taken away."

When the trials and temptations of life come, it won't be the material things that help you overcome. Instead, the courage, wisdom, strength, and understanding that God has blessed you with will be your saving grace.

Luke 12:15 "And he said unto them, Take heed, and beware of covetousness: for a man's life consisteth not in the abundance of things which he possesseth."

Never allow the material things in this world to be larger than your husband or wife. You must see the benefits of the marriage and there are many benefits. The unconditional love given in a marriage will not only bless the receiver but also the giver. When a man takes care of his body, it benefits him, so when the husband loves his wife, it brings profit to him.

Ephesians 5:28 "So ought men to love their wives as their own bodies. He that loveth his wife loveth himself."

Ephesians 5:29 "For no man ever yet hated his own flesh; but nourisheth and cherisheth it, even as the Lord the church."

The church without the Lord is nothing and to us as saints of God, the church means everything. Without the Lord being a part of our lives, it would be like living in the midst of a storm all of our days. So is it with the wife, the husband should mean everything to you. If not, you may end up single with children carrying a much greater weight.

One of the most poverty-stricken areas in today's civilization is composed of single mothers with children. There are some single women who are doing extremely well in managing their household without the man. I think it's wonderful but why spend your whole life trying to prove a point. You will end up dying long before your time is up when you take on such great responsibility. Being remembered as a hard-working woman is not better than being remembered as a woman who took care of herself, her husband, and her children as well as her household.

If the man takes a positive stand and lives according to the instructions God has given him, many things within our world would change for the better. I have said many things referring to creating a lasting marriage. Just in case you are a little confused, allow me to give some sound information. The husband must be head of the house and not only in words but his actions also. All major decisions must pass through him for his approval. In taking on the responsibility and welfare of the household, he must make the final decision to assure the well-being of the household. The wife can always give her viewpoint in a matter, but the final answer should come from the husband in whom she trusts.

God said, "If a man finds a wife, he has found a good thing." He did not say, if you find a cashier, a bus driver, business owner, doctor, or politician, He said a wife. The husband and wife must make up their minds about what is more important in the marriage, the wife or the job. Be careful how you answer that because the husband or the wife may have a different opinion.

You must keep in mind that there are so many things that go lacking when the wife works. God knew what the world would be like today, that's why He said my word would last to the end of time. In the marriage, the wife has so much laid upon her. As a man, I wonder how she gets everything done and still has time for herself. Taking care of a man and a household is not an easy task. Believe me when I say this, something is going lacking and you may not realize it until it is too late.

When the husband comes home after a day of work, he is ready to eat and relax. When the wife comes home from a day of work, her responsibilities on the job have ended but her task is now shifted to taking care of her household.

To all the wives, especially those that have a full-time job and children, I give you high praise for your hard work. Everyday you work outside of the home, your husband should give you all the respect you deserve because you are sacrificing your beauty, health, and strength trying to carry a load you were not designed for. If the wife works, it should only be to help her husband if it is required. God said He will not put any more on you than you can bear. Why put more on yourself if it is not required?

The wife is to emphasize her inner qualities, not just her outward appearance and strength. The support she gives to her husband will come from her inner strength. God's word cautions the wives against only beautifying the outside, while neglecting the mind and soul, which has a greater reward.

I Peter 3:1 "Likewise, ye wives, be in subjection to your own husband; that, if any obey not the word, they also may without the word be won by the conversation of the wives;"

I Peter 3:2 "While they behold your chaste conversation coupled with fear."

I Peter 3:3 "Whose adorning let it not be that outward adorning of plaiting of the hair, and of wearing of gold, or of putting on of apparel;"

I Peter 3:4 "But let it be the hidden man of the heart, in that which is not corruptible, even the ornament of a meek and quiet spirit, which is in the sight of God of great price."

I Peter 3:5 "For after this manner in the old time, the holy women also, who trusted in God, adorned themselves, being in subjection unto their own husbands:"

I Peter 3:6 "Even as Sarah obeyed Abraham, calling him Lord: whose daughters ye are, as long as ye do well, and are not afraid with any amazement."

To the husband and wife, you can sacrifice and do things God's way, making both of you *winners* or you can take a chance and do things your way.

"May the blessing of the Lord be with your marriage."

Chapter 7
The Responsibilities of A Husband

reat is the position which the almighty God has bestowed upon us as men. It is extremely important for a man to feel like he is head of the house in order for the plan of God to work. Men are created to respond to God's gracious word in personal love and trust. In this response only can a man be what God intended truly for him to be.

Man is offered a relationship that elevates him above everything around him through God's word of which he should live. Knowing that God has given us a responsibility of an overseer; we as men must never allow the issues we face in life to become larger than us, compromising our relationship with God.

Matthew 4:4 "But he answered and said, It is written, MAN SHALL NOT LIVE BY BREAD ALONE, BUT BY EVERY WORD THAT PROCEEDETH OUT OF THE MOUTH OF GOD."

A man truly reflects the image of God through his family and his social relationships. Our God believed in us and gave us complete control over all He created. By trusting in man, God had no problem delegating authority to him in naming every living creature. This demonstrated that man was intelligent enough to get the job done. Every name given to each creature in the beginning still stands to this day. It merely proves a man can make decisions that will last for a lifetime.

The leadership role in a family is not to be taken lightly. Every organization needs a head, and God has appointed the man head of his household. That doesn't mean that he is by any means superior over the woman. The wife is his helper and may even be smarter than the husband in some areas. This should not be considered in a negative manner because she has to be in order to be a good complement to him.

A husband and wife need to enhance each other's abilities and share each other's experiences. The husband must trust his wife and believe she can make good decisions in the area he has delegated to her. This will allow his wife to enjoy life without the stress that her husband was designed for. When a decision cannot be agreed upon, the wife must allow the husband to have the final word. If anyone refuses or disapproves of man's divine appointment, you need to take it up with God. God made the man for Himself. This being the case, the husband should have a personal relationship with Him. By the husband doing so, God can direct his path for the sake of his household.

God has given us the correct way in which the marriage must be structured. Christ is the head of the husband and the husband is the head of the wife. Now, understand that the husband is in authority but should be under the authority of God so the instructions He has given us can work to perfection.

As a husband, you must know the wife you've chosen better than anyone or anything else. It really amazes me how a man can build a machine that can go to the moon but somehow he can't love and understand his wife. The husband and wife must know each other's heart and soul. Once they are acquainted with each other, it becomes easier for the husband to manage and delegate. They must know each others actions down to the smallest of habits. Keep in mind that a marriage will never be completely in sync if you don't lay all of your cards on the table from the start. Laying the cards on the table doesn't mean telling things from the past, it means revealing only your character flaws.

When a boss has an employee, he must know what that person is capable of doing in order to affectively use that individual. The wife must give her husband the same opportunity in selecting the areas where she will be of the greatest help.

Communication will go a long way toward building trust and stability in your relationship. One of the worst things to have in a marriage is something you find out later that existed before the marriage took place. That's why it is essential to take time to get to know your spouse in the initial stages of the marriage. Early on, in some marriages, either the husband or the wife attaches themselves to other people or pastimes to where their spouse goes unnoticed. After a while, not having time for their spouse becomes a way of life.

When a couple is willing to lay down everything for each other and have clear consciences about doing so, that is true love and there is no mistake about it.

This is how friendship is established in a marriage. How many can say at this present time that they are not only husband and wife but are friends also.

Your marriage will be a work in progress at least for the first few years. You need to spend more time with each other and less time with family members, work, friends, and personal hobbies. God knew when the man and woman were created, it was possible for them to function as one if they get to know one another and if they follow His instructions. Even when two individuals appear to be compatible, without the instructions of God, functioning together can present a challenge.

Deuteronomy 24:5 "When a man hath taken a new wife, he shall not go out to war, neither shall he be charged with any business: but shall be free at home one year, and shall cheer up his wife which he hath taken."

If you have a wonderful wife, consider yourself blessed by God. Not every man that has taken on a wife has obtained the favor of the Lord. Riches may come and go but it is the Lord who gives us wisdom and understanding to select a wise and intelligent wife. Provide to her plenty of affection for standing with you. Having a wife who values you more than all of the other men she has seen and will see is a great accomplishment. Your wife must trust in you to oversee every aspect of the marriage without a shadow of a doubt. In return, she must be cared for according to the wisdom received from God.

I Corinthians 7:3 "Let the husband render unto the wife due benevolence: and likewise also the wife unto the husband."

You must remember being over a household is like Christ being over the church. As a husband, you are the strength of the marriage. When things are out of order, it's up to you to restore them back to normal. God wants the husband to function within his household with the same love and compassion as He does with the church.

The family must look to the husband for everything such as spiritual leadership, guidance, protection, support, love, truth, and well-being. There shouldn't be anything in the husband's life that he cannot put aside for his household. The child or children born will all be an extension of the husband's character. This being the case, it would be wise for the husband to stand tall in his family, not with his buddies or coworkers. Unlike with his buddies or coworkers, he has the ability to mold and shape his family.

Ephesians 5:25 "Husbands, love your wives, even as Christ also loved the church, and gave himself for it;"

Ephesians 5:26 "That he might sanctify and cleanse it with washing of water by the word,"

Ephesians 5:27 "That he might present it to himself a glorious church, not having spot, or wrinkles, or any such thing; but that it should be holy and without blemish."

Ephesians 5:28 "So ought men to love their wives as their own bodies. He that loveth his wife loveth himself."

Ephesians 5:29 "For no man ever yet hated his own flesh; but nourisheth and cherisheth it, even as the Lord the church."

Your wife will become very supportive in return for the love you give to her. You then will benefit from the love you give as she will be there to meet your every need. The more you love and respect your wife, the greater you will be loved and respected. God made it this way so that the husband profits from his love as well as the wife. It is a true saying that behind every great man there is a good woman. It is certain he did not get there without someone making sure his every need was met.

According to God, the wife will become a part of the husband and only then will you start to feel what it was like in the *Garden of Eden*. Just the thought of a marriage being the way God intended the relationship to be with both man and woman is a wonderful thing. Wives should be submissive and reverence their husbands, as Christians should submit to and worship Christ. It is a mystery how the relationship of Christ and the church is demonstrated by that of the husband and his wife.

Ephesians 5:32 "This is a great mystery: but I speak concerning Christ and the church."

Ephesians 5:33 "Nevertheless let every one of you in particular so love his wife even as himself; and the wife see that she reverence her husband."

Having the leadership role in the house, the husband must always lead by example, not by dictatorship but by democracy. Never display degrading or abusive conduct toward your wife as some men have a tendency to do today. The wife must be treated as someone that is uniquely made by God as Adam did in the Garden.

Sometimes disagreements may take place between a husband and wife or matters within the household get out of hand, leaving both the husband and the wife upset. As the leader, the husband should be the first to say sorry for letting things get out of hand. It is his job to oversee and correct all matters concerning his household. In some cases, the decision may not be correct but you must show that the decision was made with good intentions in mind. Always find a way to settle the matter in your relationship prior to falling asleep; don't let the sun go down on your anger. Anger left unattended can be explosive once it is finally addressed.

Matthew 20:27 "And whosoever will be chief among you, let him be your servant:"

As a husband, you are put in the head position by God, but in your mind, you must know that you rightfully belong there. How can you know? First of all you will have no problem serving your wife by making sure that all of her needs are fulfilled from her body to her clothing and down to the shoes she wears. If there are any spiritual, emotional, or physical concerns, she can always look to you as a support system.

The service a husband renders must extend throughout his household. If there is a child in the family and that child gets into trouble at school, it is better if the husband takes off his job to address the problem. Such an action reflects him having control of various areas within his family.

A husband must be steadfast in all he does knowing that others are depending on him and are following his lead. Ask yourself this question: What qualities or characteristics do I have that would make me want to follow myself? If it takes you awhile to answer that question or you find there is nothing as a leader you like about yourself, why would you demand or expect someone else to follow you? Your responsibility is your family. You must be willing to set the standards you expect everyone within your household to follow.

One of the first standards in a household is the husband must always maintain employment. Make a promise to your family that you will always provide for them no matter what it takes. Working is very important concerning your position in headship. The husband providing for his family against all odds sets the stage for his children later in life when or if they decide to marry. A husband should never take on the role of what society now calls a "stay-at-home dad". A true man in spirit will not accept this title. It totally goes against what God put inside of him; he will never be at peace with himself. Don't let anyone justify why it's okay to be a stay-at-home dad. In the beginning of creation,

God formed man for the purpose of working. This is his obligation until he is returned to the ground.

If a husband thinks he is a *winner* in his marriage, and he does not work, he has now been disqualified. Because as head of the house, you must run the race, not pass it to the wife, letting her work instead of you. Shame on any husband that makes his wife take on the responsibility she is not designed to handle. I know there will be many who say we have done well with the wife running the house, but I'm here to say to you a lot of things could have been better.

Don't teach your sons and daughters it's acceptable for a man not to work. The majority of the things a child learns comes from within their household environment whether good or bad. The greater part of these things is taught through the actions of the father.

Maintaining a happy and healthy relationship hinges on the husband having and keeping a job or some means of employment. Don't be deceived by others saying a woman wants a good-looking man and that's it. I truly believe a husband must be strong mentally and have the capability of being a good provider. I also strongly believe that every woman wants a husband who takes charge, but at the same time, he can be humble and sensitive. When she says, **"You are not my dad,"** you are on the right track. Every wife loves a take-charge man, whether she admits it or not. There's nothing like having the husband standing tall. Any man who sits around doing nothing and one who lets his wife walk all over him is not in the plan of God regardless of his appearance.

A man should never make excuses why he can't find work. If, as a husband, you can't find a job, you need to create one. You can't put your responsibilities on hold when you have a family depending on you for their welfare. With a willing mind, there will be some performance.

God does not measure a man's doing by conventional human standards. No one knows what goes on in the heart of man. If a man shows that he has a willing mind, God will accept that way of thinking and make a way for that man to accomplish his goals.

The husband has a great responsibility controlling and maintaining a household; it should never be handled carelessly. In **training up a child,** you initiate the process that shapes a child's life. As a father, you must understand how to equally balance love and discipline so as not to provoke your child or children into rebellion. The ideal leader is not too strict or too relaxed when dealing with those of his household.

It will take many years of sacrificing and dedication to show your children as they grow up that there is a better life other than that which they see around them on a daily basis. Within the home, every husband should be a role model for his children. Don't put the responsibility of being a role model on some individual outside of the home or some television personality. Why would you allow this to take place when you don't have any idea what kind of person these people truly represent? Give your children a clear, upfront picture of what it is to be a good man. The first few years in the early stages of their life are very important. As a father, give them some stability while they grow up. When they are all grown up or become mature adults, they will return and call you blessed for teaching them in words and in deeds.

Proverbs 22:6 "Train up a child in the way he should go: and when he is old, he will not depart from it."

A major part of a man being a good husband is how he helps his family develop a love for the things of God. As your children become familiar with the things in the world, also allow them to be knowledgeable of the things of God. Throughout their years, your kids will come to you for assistance and advice concerning many different issues in life. Always be there to provide them with an answer which they can live by. When a child is growing up, you are the greatest person in their life. I can honestly say that my children giving me respect and saying I love you is more valuable than all of my material possessions.

Proverbs 17:6 "Children's children are the crown of old men; and the glory of children are their fathers."

Marriage is the foundation from which everything is built. It is unfortunate that the love of things has changed the structure of it tremendously in these modern times. The structure as seen from God's eyes reflects the husband being the sole provider unless circumstances arise where he needs his wife's support. At that time, she may go to work to help him through whatever situation warranted her stepping in to assist him. When the matter is resolved, the wife can return to the place where she is most needed, taking care of her family.

There is no need for thousands of books to be written every year explaining how to manage a household with two incomes. The plan of God covers every detail of the marriage with simplicity. If you have read this book up to this point, there should be no misunderstanding as to who handles the money in the household. By now, you should have gathered the idea that the husband has authority over all funds within the marriage. If money seems to be an issue to the wife, she should have married her money or made a different selection during her search and before saying, **"I DO."**

In the case where the wife is working a full-time job to help with the household expenses, it's okay if this is what the husband requires. When the wife makes a sacrifice such as this, it becomes the husband's responsibility to let her know that he values and appreciates her because it is not mandatory that she does so. It is his job to carry the burden of obligations in the house, He should love his wife even more for working two full-time jobs. It holds true that the responsibility of a woman at home is more demanding than the work outside the home.

When it comes to the money, if the husband has total control of what's coming in and going out, it will benefit the marriage in more ways than one. If the wife is handling the money and paying the bills, the husband may have no idea of the available cash. As head of the house, he goes out and makes a purchase without having knowledge of his limit. The one that's not paying the bills has very little regard for what they are spending. I really think managing household finances this way is a trick of the devil because it brings about confusion.

I Corinthians 14:33 "For God is not the author of confusion, but of peace, as in all churches of the saints."

I am sure that many of the breakups in marriages are due to improper management of the money within the household. There's only one simple way to success; that's to do things in order.

The problem comes when you have the husband not willing to take all the responsibility and the wife not willing to give it up. On one hand, the husband wants to be the head but doesn't want the responsibility of paying the debts. On the other hand, the wife wants control of the money but is not willing to deal with problems that come along with it.

Many companies lose a lot due to one hand not knowing what the other hand is doing; for instance, when a purchasing manager orders supplies and the accountant pays the invoice. There may come a time an invoice may go straight to accounting and a payment is made without the item ever being requested by the individual responsible for items purchased. The company can be losing thousands of dollars and not have any knowledge of the loss.

For the best results, it is better for the husband to oversee what is being requested and be the one to pay the bills. He will watch what is being spent more closely because he is responsible for the stability of his household. Since the responsibility rests with him, there will be no one to blame when things go wrong. This method tends to make him have a faster response toward correcting the shortage. Don't take dealing with money lightly because it can become destructive. It takes time for everyone to learn God's process. So, if you, as a husband, fail in trying, God is able to pick you up. After a few times of coming up short, I guarantee he will start to understand how to become a better manager.

I Timothy 6:10 "For the love of money is the root of all evil: which while some coveted after, they have erred from the faith, and pierced themselves through with many sorrows."

There are more bitter separations in divorce court due to the fact everyone wants more than the other person because greed creeps in. This is an issue you must be concerned about. How can two people who once said they loved each other and couldn't do without one another end up fighting like cats and dogs when a breakup occurs. A husband who truly loves his wife will never mistreat her even when a separation takes place because of the unconditional love he has for her.

Remember at all times during your marriage to keep each other's family, friends, coworkers, and anyone else out of what goes on within your house. Once you involve someone on the outside, you no longer have control of how far it goes. Once something is said on the outside of the marriage, it is like opening up a pillow and driving down the interstate allowing all the feathers to disperse. You can make an attempt to gather them up but it will be practically impossible.

Outside opinions can really wreak havoc on a relationship. Don't let outside interference cause you to walk away. If you decide to walk away for whatever reason, let that decision come from the inside. Believe me, if that decision rests in your hands, you will stay together longer or maybe forever. If there are things you can't resolve between the both of you, seek counseling.

Proverbs 15:22 "Without counsel, purposes are disappointed: but in the multitude of counselors, they are established."

Man cannot comprehend God's work nor predict success; he needs to trust God for the results.

May the Lord grant you, as a leader of your house, wisdom and understanding to establish a wonderful relationship with those in your family. It doesn't matter what age you are, it's never too late to be a *winner.*

"Except the Lord build the house, they labor in vain that built it."

*The Lord is your light and your salvation; whom shall you fear?

*The Lord is the strength of your life; of whom shall you be afraid?

Chapter 8
The Responsibilities of A Wife

To the wife: trust in the almighty God to lift you up where you belong. Every woman should be looked upon as a creation that is very special and unique. It is because of her that the world continues to move forward generation after generation. She has born kings, princesses, great leaders, handsome sons, and beautiful daughters. I hope one day we all can come to the realization that as a woman created by God, she deserves the love and respect which God had in mind for her from the beginning of time.

The woman was made by the work of God's hands. She was made to execute and carry on God's greatest moment of work; the creation of man and woman. The argument still exists as to how man came about. The ability to bring forth a living being, He gave to the woman. God could have created everyone by hand but He delegated that work to the woman. To this day, no one can completely figure out or understand her throughout. With all of the technology available to man, no one can tell you how the bones grow in her womb when she is with child. No one can figure out how man was made from the dust of the earth. God has always shown His mighty works from the beginning, and He is the same God now. The woman from the beginning was created to be and will always be a special creation in life that man cannot do without.

Ecclesiastes 11:5 *"As thou knowest not what is the way of the spirit, nor how the bones do grow in the womb of her with child: even so thou knowest not the works of God who maketh all."*

You as a wife have been given a wealth of qualities that your husband and children can greatly benefit from. Hold your head up and be proud of who you are because you are unique in God's eyes. Don't allow this ever-changing world to strip you of the characteristics and qualities God bestowed upon you as a woman.

God created man strong, allowing him to perform the physical work He assigned to him. Not only did God equip the man with physical capabilities but He also made him wise and intelligent so he can execute any task God put before him. Before you say that your husband can't do something, believe in him. You have what it takes to bring out the best in him. A woman can make a man feel smart to where he feels as if he knows everything and possesses the capabilities to do all things.

Everything created, God said it was good. But when it came to man, He said it was **not good**. God's plan for man was not complete without the woman. In the beginning, man experienced loneliness without the woman, and he will continue to experience loneliness today without a woman suitable for him. Nothing in life has changed about a man and woman. We have the same need now as God saw in the beginning. Maybe the things we possess have changed but that should not play a part in the relationship because our lives don't consist of the things we possess.

People don't lose sleep for years because of a car that got repossessed or the loss of a job. On the other hand, if you have the husband of your dreams and lose him, you have lost a lot. The greatest feeling of happiness is the union of a man and a woman.

Genesis 2:18 "And the Lord God said, It is not good that the man should be alone; I will make him a help meet for him."

Genesis 2:20 "And Adam gave names to all cattle, and to the fowl of the air, and to every beast of the field; but for Adam there was not found a help meet for him."

God stated that a wife's responsibility is to be a helper to her husband. She is to aid and supply that which man cannot provide for himself. God arranged the first marriage with two people that He knew were compatible to each other. God made Adam and Eve perfect as they were made in His image and His likeness. How well matched are you to your husband?

There should be a close connection between a wife and her husband. Adam said Eve was bone of his bones because God made her from one of his ribs. God knew the bones are the essential and most durable part of the human body. In the Bible, the bones are used to describe the deepest feelings and sincerest affections.

The way in which the wife must love her husband will feel as if they were born of the same family. When God created the institution of marriage, it had to be a spiritual process. When someone gets married and later tries to separate, it becomes a difficult process. Do you really think a courthouse document can have that much of an effect on the way we think and respond? You must understand that marriage is of God. Spiritually, before God, you become one.

Your husband may be head of the household but you are the one that builds the house. It is you who is durable and stable enough to hold the household together. The wife's role in the family is extremely important and necessary because she is the one who will have the deepest emotions and affections within the home. Some may think the wife working is of more importance than the wife's contribution to the household. Nevertheless, when she spends most of her time outside of the home, everyone within her house will go lacking in one area or another.

When a husband and wife separate and there are children involved, the wife is usually left with the kids. Due to the affections God has given the woman, she is always willing to take on the responsibilities of the children regardless of the possible struggles in the future. Many men may realize she's going to have some hardships raising the children alone but it doesn't faze them at all.

For the mother to be with the children when they are young is a good thing. This is the most enjoyable time of a child's life. Many things they learn will be in the early stages of life. There is no greater experience than for a mother to be there.

There is nothing wrong with a wife going to work outside of the home if it's going to help the husband with his household obligations. When your help is required, it should be for the purpose of helping the husband. Don't view it as if you are giving assistance to take care of the household tasks. He must be responsible for the household affairs. Remember you are to help him, not take on his responsibilities. Therefore, he won't look at your help as something that will diminish his role.

Not every woman who is married is a wife. A wife doesn't come to the marriage looking for someone to take care of her. She must come to the marriage looking to serve and to take care of the others within her family. Many out there today can't honestly say at heart that they are husband and wife. In reality, they are more like business partners with equal shares. Are you a woman living with a man for the sake of having a man with you? If this is the way it is, no matter who it is, what you have gained in material possessions, or how much you have achieved, you will never be a *winner* as a person. You have lost sight of what God intended a true marriage to be.

Proverbs 14:1 "Every wise woman buildeth her house: but the foolish plucketh it down with her hands."

When a wife with a child or children says she doesn't want to be a housewife, it is very hard for me to understand. You can't find anything on the planet that is better and more enjoyable than spending time at home watching your children grow up. Over time, our society has conditioned the mind of many wives to think and feel negatively about being a housewife. You must understand that it is the wife who keeps the balance in the home. When she's unhappy, the whole house is thrown off balance.

A woman should never say, "I don't want to be *just* a housewife." The woman who makes that statement can't know what a housewife truly is. Allow me to give you a close-up view of what she is. She is considered a *domestic engineer* because she has a strong love for home life and household affairs. She manages her household in a skillful way. Her career as a housewife is never over. She will have that responsibility until our Lord Jesus says it is finished. Every other career has an age limit when most people will retire, but for the wife, the beat goes on. She will be teaching and embracing not only her children but others also. There is no other job given under heaven that requires such a great commitment. It should be an honor for the wife to take on this position that the almighty God entrusts her with.

How can one say that being at home is boring and laid-back? The duties a wife must perform are never ending. She must be capable of multi-tasking and she can never stop learning how to bring balance to her household. For the wife, learning is a lifelong process because the household will forever create new challenges for her. Any day of the week, she can become a dentist, doctor, counselor, comforter, chef, babysitter, nurse, educator, taxi driver, dishwasher, hair stylist, friend, cheerleader, and the list goes on day after day depending on the situation.

For me as a husband, life at home was very enjoyable due to my wife being at home. My wife did all of the things listed above and more. Regardless of the disagreements she and my adult children have, I will never allow them to disrespect her due to all of the labor she put in when they were growing up. To see a child respond back to their parents in a negative way, especially to the mother, is heartbreaking. This should not be allowed because of all the love and care she has given throughout the years. She was the one who got up in the middle of the night when they were sick, not me.

When the wife is at home, the husband never has to deal with the small matters of the household. He will be free to focus on the wife and the well-being of the family.

When a man has a good wife who doesn't mind being very supportive in their relationship, he can get a lot of things accomplished. Every day that I came home from work, the house was always pleasant. The kids were in their rooms, soft music was playing on the radio, and everything was in order. After I would unwind and settle down, the kids came out and smothered me. When they were growing up, we had a wonderful time because they had never seen me uptight or upset from a hard day's work. Because of the way things were handled, at this present time, my children and I are the best of friends. This was one of the methods she created as a housewife that worked well for me. In the beginning, setting the stage in my life was very important, and today I feel I can accomplish anything that I set my mind to do.

Proverb 12:4 "A virtuous woman is a crown to her husband: but she that maketh ashamed is as rottenness in his bones."

Take a look around, almost certainly you will see many mothers and their adult children unable to get along. This is a result of her having to work and not being able to provide all of the *little* things needed to raise them from a child. She is working and providing gifts to show her love but love and discipline go together. Cracks are then created in the adult relationship of a mother and child because one or the other went lacking in their bonding process during childhood.

One of the wife's first steps in following a perfect plan for a wonderful marriage is submitting to her husband. Many people all over the world frown on the fact that a woman must submit to the man. It is part of the woman's makeup from God. Submitting is part of her design and not submitting is telling God you don't like and appreciate the way He made you. God's intention in making the woman was that she would add to her husband's life as they become one.

Wifely submission should not be sternly enforced. It must be something a wife is willing to do on her own for the blessings of God to freely flow. I found that when a woman submits to the Lord, she will have no problem submitting to her husband. It goes without saying that when she submits to her husband, she will be delighted to submit to the Lord.

Don't worry about submitting to your husband if he ends up mistreating you. If he wants God to be just and fair with him, he will be fair toward his wife. This is a heavenly submission that a woman gives, but it is only given provided the husband's directions are in the fear of God or at least in line with His will. When your husband is out of line with the will of God, you must be careful in submitting to him.

There was a husband and wife in the Bible named Ananias and Sapphira. They sold one of their possessions and kept part of the money. The husband did not want to tell the full price they received from the selling of it. His wife, being submissive to him, agreed with him to tell a lie to the apostles. When the husband told the lie, he fell dead. When the wife, being submissive to her husband, was asked, "Did you sell the land for so much?" and she then gave the answer she and her husband had agreed upon, she fell down and died.

Acts 5:1 "BUT a certain man named Ananias, with Sapphira his wife, sold a possession,"

Acts 5:2 "And kept back part of the price, his wife also being privy to it, and brought a certain part, and laid it at the apostles' feet."

Acts 5:3 "But Peter said, Ananias, why hath Satan filled thine heart to lie to the Holy Ghost, and to keep back part of the price of the land?"

Acts 5:4: "While it remained, was it not thine own? and after it was sold, was it not in thine own

power? Why hast thou conceived this thing in thine heart? Thou hast not lied unto men, but unto God."

Acts 5:5 "And Ananias hearing these words fell down, and gave up the ghost: and great fear came on all them that heard these things."

Acts 5:6 "And the young men arose, wound him up, and carried him out, and buried him."

Acts 5:7 "And it was about the space of three hours after, when his wife, not knowing what was done, came in."

Acts 5:8 "And Peter answered unto her, Tell me whether ye sold the land for so much? And she said, Yea, for so much."

Acts 5:9 "Then Peter said unto her, How is it that ye have agreed together to tempt the Spirit of the Lord? Behold, the feet of them which have buried thy husband are at the door, and shall carry thee out."

Acts 5:10 "Then fell she down straightway at his feet, and yielded up the ghost: and the young men came in, and found her dead, and, carrying her forth, buried her by her husband."

Acts 5:11 "And great fear came upon all the church, and upon as many as heard these things."

God does not judge every sin with death. But you do not want your blessings and prayers hindered. He is a personal savior. I hereby caution you to be careful how and when you submit concerning the Lord.

Colossians 3:18 "Wives, submit yourselves unto your own husband, as it is fit in the Lord."

God created the wife to take care of her husband. A good wife will elevate her husband. Her love and care for him is more important than outward beauty. When a man walks out in public, everyone should be able to tell if he is a single or married man. If you can't tell, some wife somewhere is not taking care of her husband. He should be well groomed, his clothes always neat, his nails manicured, and so on. A wife must know what's going on within her home at all times.

Proverbs 19:14 "House and riches are the inheritance of fathers: and a prudent wife is from the Lord."

It is great when you know someone is looking out for you. I was a supervisor of a manufacturing facility within the city for many years. My wife became accustomed to me wearing a long-sleeve white shirt to work every day. Everyone who knew me in the industry got familiar with the white shirt with the sleeves rolled up. After working in the same environment for so long, the way I dressed for work was a way of life. One day, the owners decided to relocate the company from the city to a rural area where a white shirt wasn't popular.

During the first two years, everything went well. Then one Friday, my boss came into my office and told me, "Have your work clothes on when you come in Monday morning."

While driving home, I began thinking I had on my work clothes. I couldn't understand what he was talking about because I dressed the same as I had done for many years.

When I made it to work on Monday, the first thing he said was, "I told you to wear your work clothes."

In my mind, I was thinking, "What is this man talking about?"

For the next few months, every day he put me on the shop floor working with the guys until I stopped wearing white shirts due to the oil and dirt stains constantly ruining them.

Over a period of time, I began to dress like everyone else. My attire completely changed. One morning, I was heading out to work and my wife came to the door.

Before she said goodbye, she said, "Wallace, I like who you are and don't let anyone change you."

It was as if the light came back on. For a while, I was allowing someone to slowly change the way I thought. My friends and everyone around me never said a word. It was a good thing that my wife pleasantly informed me of what was going on.

The Bible states two are better than one, when he falls he has someone to lift him up. I went back into the house and changed clothes putting on a long-sleeve white shirt and rolling the sleeves up. I went to work from that day on refusing to let my boss change me. There were many white shirts destroyed, but over a period of time, my boss realized that he could not change who I was. Thanks to my wife for looking out for my best interests.

Many wives have lost sight of their husband because they are too busy taking care of themselves. They don't have time for the one that should mean the most to them. God created you to help the husband, and once you finish taking care of him, then spend some time on yourself. Looking after the husband's appearance is something only a true wife can do. The woman has a divine implanted desire to have a good appearance. This is a perfect example where two become one; now she can keep him looking good. A desire to look good is one of the many qualities a wife brings to the marriage. There is no price you can put on the attention you give to your husband.

Before you get married, as a single woman, you get the opportunity to care for yourself and the things you love. When you get married, you must now care for the family and the things they love. If you can't put your family first, you should have remained a single woman.

The quality of a wife found in the Bible is what every man should love for his wife to pattern herself after. God unfolds twenty-two qualities about an excellent wife. Each verse highlights a different quality of her. A good wife is rare to find because she has to demonstrate the principles of wisdom and understanding in her home. A wife must have peace within her so she can execute the understanding given by God which will be her strength in the time of need.

The Virtuous Woman

Proverbs 31:10 "Whom can find a virtuous woman? For her price is far above rubies."

She is rare and hard to find; her worth cannot be determined.

Proverbs 31:11 "The heart of her husband doth safely trust in her, so that he shall have no need of spoil."

Her husband can trust her with everything he has, including all of his personal and business affairs.

Proverbs 31:12 "She will do him good and not evil all the days of her life."

She will give him continuous love and respect for a lifetime.

Proverbs 31:13 "She seeketh wool, and flax, and worketh willingly with her hands."

She is hard-working and doesn't mind because her husband has set a good example.

Proverbs 31:14 "She is like the merchants' ship; she bringeth her food from afar."

She is economic and makes the best of what is available.

Proverbs 31:15 "She riseth also while it is yet night, and giveth meat to her household, and a portion to her maidens."

She sacrifices herself for her family and distributes the necessities to all within the household.

Proverbs 31:16 "She considereth a field, and buyeth it: with the fruit of her hands she planteth a vineyard."

She is creative and is always thinking about what's best for her family.

Proverbs 31:17 "She girdeth her loins with strength, and strengtheth her arms."

She strengthens herself mentally to handle family issues that may arise and is also willing to work hard.

Proverbs 31:18 "She perceiveth that her merchandise is good: her candle goeth not out by night."

She knows what she is working for and is willing to work all night if it takes that.

Proverbs 31:19 "She layeth her hands to the spindle, and her hands hold the distaff."

Repetitive work never seems to be a discouragement to her.

Proverbs 31:20 "She stretcheth out her hand to the poor; yea, she reacheth forth her hands to the needy."

She is very sympathetic to the poor and generous to those who are in need.

Proverbs 31:21 "She is not afraid of the snow for her household: for all her household are clothed with scarlet."

She will always be ahead of what is facing her family so she can get things in place where they're needed when the time draws near.

Proverbs 31:22 "She maketh herself coverings of tapestry; her clothing is silk and purple."

She is not cheap. She makes her clothes from the best materials. She will set standards for others to follow.

Proverbs 31:23 "Her husband is known in the gates, when he sitteth among the elders of the land."

She marries a leader, and he is known by the support she gives him. She brings out the best in him, making him look and feel like a leader.

Proverbs 31:24 "She maketh fine linen, and selleth it; and delivereth girdles unto the merchant."

She is a businesswoman and she knows how to help her husband if it is required.

Proverbs 31:25 "Strength and honor are her clothing; and she shall rejoice in time to come."

She is strong and has great integrity. She is not easily influenced by the conditions that surround her. She has faith that things will always get better.

Proverbs 31:26 "She opened her mouth with wisdom; and in her tongue is the law of kindness."

She is an example to all who are around her, in words, in conversation, in love, in spirit, and in belief.

Proverbs 31:27 "She looketh well to the ways of her household, and eateth not the bread of idleness."

She will find something to do within her household before she sits and does nothing without a reason.

Proverbs 31:28 "Her children arise up, and call her blessed; her husband also, and he praiseth her."

Her husband and children can never say and do enough to show their appreciation for her undying service to the family.

Proverbs 31:29 "Many daughters have done virtuously, but thou excellest them."

She is not content being just an average woman.

Proverb 31:30 "Favor is deceitful, and beauty is vain: but a woman that feareth the Lord, she shall be praised."

She is most happy with loving God rather than being caught up in looks and favor.

Proverb 31:31 "Give her of the fruit of her hands; and let her own works praise her in the gates."

I am sure that her husband gives her all the praise she needs. Because of her hard work and dedication to the home, she is worthy of praise. She, being able to agree with him when she disagrees, will give him the courage to step out by faith to fulfill his role as head of the house. When he makes a mistake, she will never criticize his efforts but give him support for trying. If there is love and respect between the husband and wife, it will have a positive effect on the children. Our sons and daughters will learn to respect the opposite sex, which will decrease many of the problems facing our children today.

God has given us the perfect instructions and only when we use them can we reach the ultimate goal of becoming a winner.

May our Lord and Savior give you, as a wife, the will to succeed and be happy.

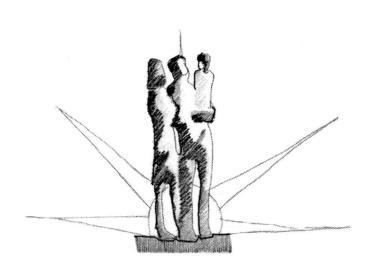

Chapter 9
A Happy Home

God established the first family because He knew it would be the greatest joy of accomplishment a man and woman could receive during their lifetime on earth. With God being the creator of the family, I'm sure He placed Himself in the center position. He is the only one who can create perfect harmony between two individuals. This was not done for the purpose of controlling the marriage but more so to guide it. When things don't go smoothly, He can always give you the knowledge required to get back on track.

Hopefully you have read and understood chapters one through eight. God has shown you the *way* in which the home should operate. He has given you the *truth* in His words which will lead and guide you. Now it is your choice whether or not the information written in this book will become your *life*.

We must consider God's plan for the family. Any other plan without God included will fail in one way or another. There is a parable written in the Bible that will give us a clear understanding of how plans fail without Him.

Luke 12:16 *"And he spake a parable unto them, saying, The ground of a certain rich man brought forth plentifully:"*

Luke 12:17 *"And he thought within himself, saying, What shall I do, because I have no room where to bestow my fruit?"*

Luke 12:18 *"And he said, This will I do: I will pull down my barns, and build greater; and there will I bestow all of my fruits and my goods."*

Luke 12:19 *"And will say to my soul, Soul, thou hast much goods laid up for many years; take thine ease, eat, drink, and be merry."*

Luke 12:20 *"But God said unto him, Thou fool, this night thy soul shall be required of thee: then whose shall those things be, which thou has provided?"*

He was a fool, for he thought he knew something that he didn't. He presumed he had the resources to control his destiny. Omitting God is merely bad planning. Many today are planning their future without considering God in their plan.

In this book is found the purpose for marriage and the responsibilities of the husband and wife within the marriage. If you are willing to change or adjust, a happy home can be yours. You must have an open and willing mind to change whatever may need changing. Having a happy home depends greatly on your ability to accept the truth and make a change.

In a marriage, the most important commodity within the household is your spouse and children if there are any. There shall be nothing inside or outside of your home more important than those of your household. When both the husband and wife realize that no one and nothing is before them, they will help the other accomplish everything in life they have the desire to achieve. Our world is ever changing and presenting new challenges. As a result, there will be many occasions where you will be confronted with an issue and have to make a decision about what means the most to you. If society doesn't make an effort to change, marriage as we know it will be a thing of the past.

Most individuals who walk down the aisle for marriage go with the thought that it is going to last a lifetime. They don't have the preconceived notion that it's only going to last six months, a year, or possibly five years. If this was so, they would have already prepared themselves for when it comes to an end. This is not the case in many situations because when the marriage ends, the hard feelings begin to surface and malice creeps in.

In many cases today, simply living together appears to be a better option just due to the fact no one knows what to expect in a marriage. With so much misunderstanding, it is no wonder many marriages seem to be balls of confusion.

If you have ever been married, you will be able to relate to the following flashback. Allow me to take you back to your wedding day just as the ceremony began. For the first second or two, God gave you a glimpse of how beautiful your marriage could be. Those few moments are like no other experience you've witnessed. There is very little they can be compared to. Just think for a moment. What if the marriage can remain that way for a lifetime?

God allowed us to feel what the marriage was like in the beginning, then He put the decision in our hands. It is achievable if we follow His instructions. The choice is up to you. Whatever you allow, God will allow. Your marriage can be like the first few seconds of the ceremony every day. Have you ever noticed when a marriage is over, the wife that once was will not give up her wedding pictures even though each person has moved on with their life? To the woman, that was the highlight of her life, and something she will never forget despite the end result of her marriage.

Without God, it's like you are starting a marital journey without getting the map from the one who created the path for marriage. Many start out great but end in disaster. You can be doing fantastically, but if you make one bad turn, your journey will come to an end. Don't let yourself be a victim of this circumstance. Take as much time as you can to get information concerning one of the most complex institutions there is. It is wise to find out what is on the road ahead. You owe it to the one who loves you the most because they are willing to be with you for a lifetime.

Having a wonderful relationship is a clear-cut issue that must be decided. You don't have to pray about it or fast for it. The only thing you have to do is make a decision to either follow the plan God has laid out for us or walk away.

In the Bible, there is a great passage concerning a rich young ruler who had to make a similar decision.

Mark 10:17 "And when he was gone forth into the way, there came one running, and kneeled to him, and asked him, Good Master, what shall I do that I may inherit eternal life?"

Mark 10:18 "And Jesus said unto him, Why callest thou me good? There is none good but one, that is, God."

Mark 10:19 "Thou knowest the commandments, DO NOT COMMIT ADULTERY, DO NOT KILL, DO NOT STEAL, DO NOT BEAR FALSE WITNESS, Defraud not, HONOR THY FATHER AND MOTHER."

Mark 10:20 "And he answered and said unto him, Master, all these have I observed from my youth."

Mark 10:21 "Then Jesus beholding him loved him, and said unto him, One thing thou lackest: go thy way, sell whatsoever thou hast, and give to the poor, and thou shalt have treasure in heaven: and come, take up the cross, and follow me."

Mark 10:22 "And he was sad at the saying, and went away grieved: for he had great possessions."

Mark 10:21 "And Jesus looked round about, and saith unto his disciples, How hardly shall they that have riches enter into the kingdom of God!"

Notice in the following verse what the kingdom of God is. The young man walks away from the opportunity to have all the inward blessings that could have made him whole. God is offering us the same blessing. This is to experience what the kingdom of God is like here on earth. God will never be mad at what you are allowing to happen to yourself. The wisdom of God is here for the taking but the decision to take it is yours.

Romans 14:17 "For the kingdom of God is not meat and drink; but righteousness, and peace, and joy in the Holy Ghost."

Many today speak as the rich young ruler in saying, the Lord is good. If God told people what they needed to do right now to create a happy home, how many will begin to justify their current state and why it would be impossible for them to do so? Husbands and wives all over the country would be saying, "I'm doing my part in the relationship." Maybe you are doing a wonderful job within your marriage, but at the same time, you could be operating outside of the plan of God.

When the young ruler said to *JESUS, "I* have kept everything that you said from my youth." He was letting God know that what he was doing should have been sufficient. If *JESUS* said to you right now, "Have you done everything right within your relationship?" What would you say? Would you recite a list of things you've done over a period of time? Just as *JESUS* looked at the young man and had compassion on him, He will deal with you the same because He knows there may be something keeping you from having total happiness.

All of the wealth and fame a person may have cannot fulfill the inward desire to be happy. Adam had loneliness in the beginning that only God could fix. God knew exactly what Adam needed. I'm sure when He presented Eve, it was a joyous time. Remember, there was nothing around to separate, distract, or distort Adam and Eve's view of each other. Their happiness came from each other without interference. There have been so many changes since then. We need help more now than ever with relationship issues.

When *JESUS* said to the rich young ruler, "One thing you lack: go your way, sell whatever you have, and give it to the poor, and you shall have treasures in heaven." *JESUS* told him to take up his cross and follow Him. The young ruler was sad at the request of *JESUS* and went away grieved because he was very rich and did not want to part with his possessions. *JESUS* knew wherever his treasure was there will his heart be also. The same applies to you. Where is your treasure at this time?

According to the word of God, man and woman have been given a perfect plan in which to live concerning marriage. God is saying to you as He did to the rich ruler get rid of whatever's holding you back from enjoying total happiness within your marriage. As a man, don't let your lack of confidence in managing a household force you to walk away grieved as the young man did. God loves you and He knows what you must do in order to have complete happiness. As a woman, don't allow the fact of man being the head of the house force you to walk away unhappy. This is the Lord's doing, and it should be considered marvelous in our eyes.

How can you achieve peace, joy, and total happiness in your home if you have something with a greater value than your husband or wife? You can't! That is why the young ruler walked away. He valued his possessions more than he valued following *JESUS*.

If you have made a lifelong commitment, it is imperative for the almighty God to find favor with your marriage. It is God who delegates to the husband what he must do and it is the husband that delegates what the wife must do. This order from God will allow us to move on to perfection.

I Corinthians 11:7 "For a man indeed ought not to cover his head, forasmuch as he is the image and glory of God: but the woman is the glory of man."

A happy home is the ultimate goal of any married couple. But God has given us a divine order which we must follow to receive the fullness of our relationship, wherein a man is excited to be a man and a woman is glad to be a woman. A good relationship will help develop both the husband and the wife in more ways than you can ever imagine. There is nothing greater on earth to God than for a husband and wife to live joyfully.

Ecclesiastes 9:9 "Live joyfully with the wife whom thou lovest all the days of the life of thy vanity, which he hath given thee under the sun, all the days of thy vanity: for that is thy portion in this life, and in thy labor which thou takest under the sun."

Making a wise decision in your relationship can be the key to your success. The Bible speaks about how God made a promise to Israel that He would come down, deliver them out of the hands of the Egyptians, and bring them out of bondage unto a good land that was large and flowed with milk and honey.

At no time did God say it was going to be easy receiving the blessings He promised. Even as God led the way to the promised land, there were some who murmured against Him. The Lord's anger was aroused against Israel because of the murmuring and complaining. God then made them wander in the wilderness forty years until the entire rebellious generation and those who had done evil in His sight were consumed. God wants us to have the best in our relationships. The land that flowed with milk and honey is compared to God's kind of paradise.

We can have the same kind of paradise within our homes if we allow the plan of God to take its course in the family. Just as Israel murmured I know there will be many that will turn over every rock on the planet to find a reason why the instructions of God won't work for them. I hope many will not wander aimlessly for years and never reach the point of happiness in trying to go another way.

Every household has the same opportunity to be a happy home. No family has the edge within the institution of marriage. Rich or poor, small or great, short or tall, black or white; we are all the same in God's eyes. You can be in a rich neighborhood or a poor neighborhood; it doesn't matter because man's ability cannot guarantee winning results. Everybody is equal before God, rich and poor alike. What matters is the understanding that is applied behind the walls. God is the source from which true wisdom and help is found.

Jeremiah 9:23 "Thus saith the Lord, Let not the wise man glory in his wisdom, neither let the mighty man glory in his might, let not the rich man glory in his riches:"

Jeremiah 9:24 "But let him that glorieth glory in this, that he understandeth and knoweth me, that I am the Lord which exercise lovingkindness, judgment, and righteousness, in the earth: for in these things, I delight, saith the Lord."

God said in the home there is no law against love, joy, peace, long-suffering, gentleness, goodness, faith, meekness, and temperance. There is no limit on how much of these you can give in your home. There is no law to stop you from giving too much love. Have you ever heard of someone getting arrested for loving too much?

Many of the qualities that should exist in the home are as follows: *Love* is willing and giving of oneself for the benefit of the family without thought of receiving anything in return. True love cannot be destroyed by death or the grave. It burns like a fire that cannot be put out and it cannot be bought for a price. *Joy* is gladness of heart to behold your family. *Peace* is harmony within the family, freeing them from worry and fear. *Long-suffering* is having patience with all that are in the household. *Gentleness* is always being kind. *Goodness* is showing compassion within the household. *Faith* is assuring the family that you're dependable. *Meekness* is courtesy and giving consideration in the relationship. *Temperance* is having self-control concerning all things.

Song of Solomon 8:7 "Many waters cannot quench love, neither can the floods drown it: if a man would give all the substance of his house for love, it would utterly be contemned."

It takes everyone within the family to build a happy home, starting at the T-O-P! God has entrusted the husband with leading his family. The husband, being head of the household, is completely responsible for the protection and comfort of his family. He has a "*no-escape clause*" in his relationship with God that does not allow him to abort his responsibilities. It states he must work. It is the husband's responsibility to execute the standards within the household. As head of the house, you can never be afraid of the different challenges that face you daily. Taking on responsibilities as a man will only make you stronger but will weaken a woman over time. It is a God-given design that not some but all men have.

There is a wonderful account of victory in the Bible that supports the above statement. David was a young lad who watched after his father's sheep. As a shepherd, he had the responsibility of protecting the sheep from any unforeseen danger. With responsibility comes challenges. One day, David was keeping his father's sheep when a lion and a bear came and took a sheep out of the flock. David then went after the lion and struck him and delivered the sheep out of his mouth. When the lion rose up against David, he killed the lion. David slew both the lion and the bear thus preparing him for any challenge facing him later in life.

A much greater challenge came when David faced Goliath, but David was not afraid. David stood on his victorious moments and said, "The Lord delivered me out of the paw of the lion and out of the paw of the bear, He will deliver me out of the hands of Goliath." David's confidence grew from his experience of previous deliverances.

As a shepherd, David began demonstrating his courage by killing the lion and the bear that attacked the flock. But he became a leader when he killed the giant, Goliath. Later, David went on to become King. As the responsibility grew, he also grew as a man. Everything that you handle as head of the house will only make you stronger. When you are a leader, you must stand up against anything that faces those under your leadership. I know your wife and children will be forever grateful.

The husband is the major player in constructing a happy home. He must not misuse or abuse his authority. When there is business to be done concerning the home, let the husband step up to the plate. He must manage his family rightly. Every way that is good and right for the family must be set by example.

I Timothy 3:4 "One that ruleth well his own house, having his children in subjection with all gravity."

If there is a disagreement with the wife, don't try to correct the matter in front of the children. You don't want the children deciding which parent they favor from your conversation. When the children need discipline, the husband and wife should never show disagreement when it comes to what's right and wrong.

For the record, it is a disgrace for a man to hit or beat on a woman. I would love to see the husband who commits such crimes later stand before God trying to explain the reason for hitting and beating on His special creation. What are you saying to God when you abuse a woman? You don't like what He created? The scriptures had stated that the woman is the weaker one; therefore, there is nothing to prove by using physical force. Remember, according to chapter five, she was your selection in the search, so why take it out on her when you were the one that made the mistake. All the years of my marriage, I have never once put my hands on my wife. For that reason, my daughters will make sure their future husbands keep their hands to themselves.

For many husbands, trying to balance the responsibilities and give love is not an easy task. Some men are not good at saying, "I love you," which is something a woman loves to hear. When a husband meets all of the wife's and children's needs, he expresses his love by letting no one in his house go lacking in any area. A husband will receive from his wife what he gives to her. If he respects her, she will give him respect in return. It is very important that the wife allow the husband to be the head because she only has to give back what the husband gives to her. He has a great responsibility in overseeing the home and should have someone helpful by his side.

God expects the husbands to dwell with their wives according to the knowledge they received from His words, giving honor unto them, as unto the weaker one, and as being recipients together of the blessing of life, that their desires be granted unto them.

There is nothing greater than for the Lord to say to you as a good man, a good husband, and a good father, *"Well done, my son."*

The wife is second in command. Wives don't get upset because you were placed in order according to the will of God. Your greatest purpose is to be a helper to your husband as needed. As a wife, your responsibility is to uphold every standard that is put in place by the husband as a guide for the family. The wife, being able to submit, will allow the husband to execute his responsibilities with authority. If he says, "What's done in this house stays in this house," you must keep relatives and family members out of your household affairs. Your household affairs are your business. There is only one head and that's the husband, and he does not need any outside interference. The only time one should get advice from the outside is when they are getting help from a counselor only. Your marriage does not need help from a friend or relatives. Be willing to communicate concerning all matters with each other.

Wives, if you don't have children, spend more time looking after the well-being and care of your husband. You are the only creation that God made that can make a man feel like he can walk on water.

But to the wives who have children, you can never give them enough love and guidance. I get no greater joy than to see a mother giving her children a lot of affection.

Take notice of the following scripture; which parent is brought to shame? A mother must do her job!

Proverbs 29:15: "The rod and reproof give wisdom: but a child left to himself bringeth his <u>mother</u> to shame."

When it comes to disciplining the children, they will most of the time understand the reason for the correction because they are surrounded by good. Knowing what good is, the child will know within themselves when they are out of line. There is a thin line between right and wrong, but a good mother will have no problem keeping balance between showing love and discipline. This balance will bring about obedience in the children.

Every child that you have is a blessing from the Lord. You must treat your child or children as if they are a special gift from God, because it will only be for a short time. Teach your children well because a child in the right environment will bring you joy and protection.

Genesis 33:4 "And Esau ran to meet him, and embraced him, and fell on his neck, and kissed him: and they wept."

Genesis 33:5 "And he lifted up his eyes, and saw the woman and her children; and said, Who are those with thee? And he said, The children which God hath graciously given thy servant."

To all mothers, this is not a commandment of the Lord but from me by the spirit of *Christ*. It would be better if you could remain at home while your children are young because you have only been granted by God a short time to be ruler over them. I'm not saying they will lose respect for you when they are older but the wants and needs in their life will change. I always encourage a parent to start preparing themselves at least a year early for when that child leaves home. You look at your beautiful child and wish they could be with you forever. But yes, they will leave home one day. Many parents don't prepare themselves for that day, and when, at a moment's notice, that child decides to leave, it brings tears to their eyes. In her heart, she will wonder where has the time gone and if she did as much as she could to prepare them for their future.

Your children will grow up and become one of you; an adult who can run their own home. When that time comes, you must be careful because you will find yourself not dealing with a child but an adult. At this point in their lives, you have lost your opportunity to treat them like a child. God set a perfect example in this area when He had to deal with Adam and Eve. God said, "They have become one of us, a god, to know good and evil." After this took place, it was time for man to go because the privileges and responsibilities changed at this point, so shall it be with your children. God said, "Once man reaches my level, it's time for them to go and make it on their own."

Genesis 3:22 "And the Lord God said, Behold, the man is become one of us, to know good and evil: and now, lest he be put forth his hand, and take also of the tree of life, and eat, and live for ever."

Genesis 3:23 "Therefore, the Lord God sent him forth from the garden of Eden, to till the ground from whence he was taken."

Having young or older children in the family will play a role in having a happy home. There are many marriages torn apart at this very moment due to the actions of the children within the home. If the husband doesn't handle matters concerning the children when need be, it can spell disaster in the marriage. When the children are living at home, the older they become, the more wisdom and knowledge the parents need in order to have harmony with them. There are many parents who have worked very hard to achieve what they have. Children who disrespect their parents can destroy within minutes everything they have built.

When your children were small, they had many privileges and responsibilities they could do, but not as an adult. When my son was only a kid, he had the responsibility of taking out the trash. When he became an adult, it's not the same telling him to take the trash out. If he was trained well as a child, I will no longer have to ask. The education in the home will help form the child's position throughout his or her lifetime.

Ephesians 6:4 "And, ye fathers, provoke not your children to wrath: but bring them up in the nurture and admonition of the Lord."

It will be a good thing to have God standing behind the parent's rearing and teaching of their children as the chief teacher in educating the child. Parents, it is such a great undertaking to go at it alone.

I know that some of you are saying, "Hurry up and get to sex in a relationship." First, we must get the house in order, so you can enjoy the pleasure of having sex with the person you love and respect. Many couples have allowed the sexual part to dominate the relationship. Sex in the marriage should only be a small part of the process of building a happy home. Don't let sex become bigger than all the things you do for your mate, because it will be simple for them to walk out for someone else. In our day and time, intimacy has changed lives all over the world. Many experiences have been good and many bad. But for now, we will refrain from that discussion before someone allows it to ruin the whole book. Our minds are overpowered in many cases with the conversation of sex. Look for this topic in the **next issue**.

A well-balanced household is required from start to finish. If things are done in the right order, the home can and will always be a happy home.

If you take heed to the advice given in this book, the Lord will bless you to be a *WINNER* in your relationship.

I don't know about you, but I am a winner, and I pray you can experience what it is to be one also.

About the Author

As a twenty-two year teacher of a Christian Ministry, Wallace Welch has been highly respected and admired for his ability to lead in all aspects of life. Wallace is a speaker and writer who is gifted to apply ancient biblical truths to a modern way of life. By no means does he limit his teaching to a platform or printed pages. His life is a great example to all.

Printed in the United States
31680LVS00002BC/82-408